# HENRY FONDA

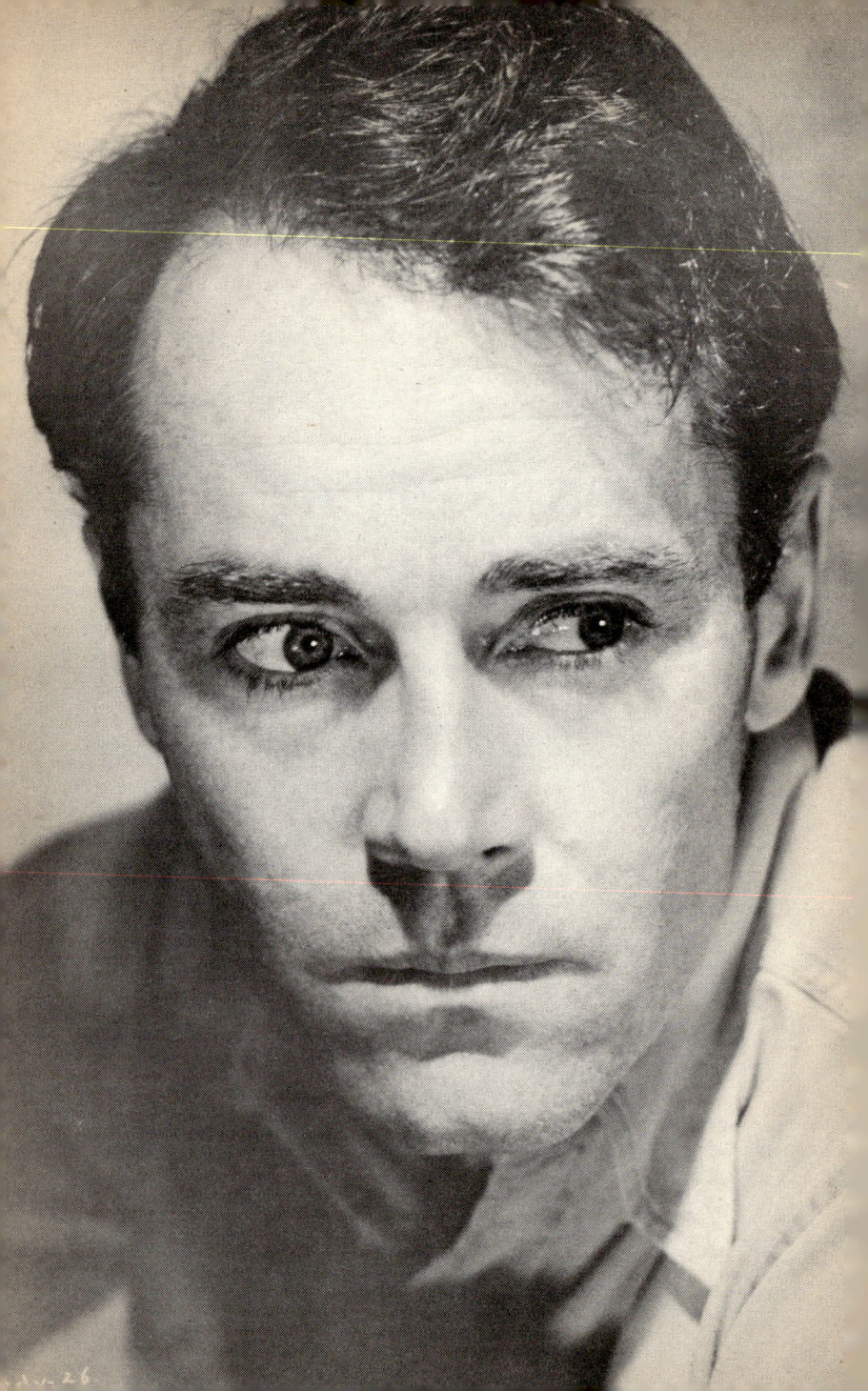

# HENRY FONDA

*A Pyramid Illustrated History of the Movies*

by
**MICHAEL KERBEL**

*General Editor:* **TED SENNETT**

PUBLICATIONS
NEW YORK

To Diane

**HENRY FONDA**
*A Pyramid Illustrated History of the Movies*

Copyright © 1975 by Pyramid Communications, Inc.

All rights reserved. No part of this publication may be reproduced or transmitted in any form or by any means, electronic or mechanical, including photocopy, recording, or any information storage and retrieval system, without permission in writing from the publisher.

Pyramid edition published July 1975

ISBN 0-515-03738-9

Library of Congress Catalog Card Number: 75-4428

Printed in the United States of America

Pyramid Books are published by Pyramid Communications, Inc. Its trademarks, consisting of the word "Pyramid" and the portrayal of a pyramid, are registered in the United States Patent Office.

Pyramid Communications, Inc., 919 Third Avenue, New York, N.Y. 10022

Photographs: Jerry Vermilye, The Memory Shop, Cinemabilia, Movie Star News

(graphic design by anthony basile)

# ACKNOWLEDGMENTS

I should like to thank Bea Herrmann of *Macmillan Audio Brandon* and Pat Moore of *United Artists 16*, who generously allowed me to screen many Henry Fonda films.

I am grateful to Andrew Sarris and Richard Corliss, who first gave me the opportunity to write film criticism, and whose own writings have been inspiring; and to my editor, Ted Sennett, who has guided me through two books.

My sincere thanks to the following, who aided me in the preparation of this book: Mary Balgach, John Foster, Larry French, Bill Kenly, Howard Mandelbaum, Bertie Musicus, Michael Ryan, Susan Steinbach, William Walton, and the staffs of the Museum of Modern Art Film Study Center and the Lincoln Center Library of the Performing Arts.

And I will always be in debt to the following, for their encouragement, their friendship, and their extreme tolerance in listening to my endless complaints: Anna Bass, Warren Bass, Keith Bird, Lelija Bird, Mary Corliss, Robert Edelstein, Diane and Albert Galimidi, Stephen Harvey, Foster Hirsch, Arlee Siegel, Emily Sieger, Francine Skurnick, Mark Zucker, and, above all, my parents.

Once again, I wish especially to thank my friend Charles Silver, for providing much information and arranging the screening of many films, and for his infinite generosity and patience.

——Michael Kerbel

# CONTENTS

A Man of Integrity .................................................10

From the Farmland to *The Farmer* ...............................17

Plowboys and Playboys ...........................................23

Mr. Fonda and Mr. Ford ..........................................45

Snakes, Simpletons, and Social Significance ......................64

Stage Interlude ...................................................84

Law, Politics, and Father Figures ................................88

Heroes and Anti-heroes .........................................112

Bibliography ....................................................142

The Films of Henry Fonda .....................................143

The Broadway Appearances of Henry Fonda ....................152

Index ............................................................153

# A MAN OF INTEGRITY

If one had to characterize Henry Fonda in a single word, it might be "integrity." As Peter Bogdanovich has observed, "When Henry Fonda says something, you believe it. . . . This is a quality of real stars and no one has it more than Fonda." There's a transcendent honesty and sincerity about him, whether he's playing a sheriff or an outlaw, a lawyer or a criminal, a college teacher or a farmer, a president or a priest.

This stems largely from his background. He was born and raised in Nebraska, the nation's heartland and center of the Bible Belt, and his origin has remained with him. It has helped make his characters appealing because of a traditional and enduring American belief in the virtues of small-town or country life, in the integrity of the soil.

The myth has been an essential part of much of American literature, thought and popular culture —from the writings of Jefferson and Thoreau to the appeal of country music and "The Waltons." In films, directors like D.W. Griffith, Henry King, John Ford, King Vidor, and Frank Capra have extolled, and actors like Gary Cooper, James Stewart, and Fonda have embodied, the supposed values of rural America.

At the center of the myth is the heroic, self-reliant farmer, the mainstay of America until the industrialization of the late nineteenth and twentieth centuries, and idealized thereafter. The farmer represented the Puritan ethic of hard, honest work and clean, upright living, and he realized the promise of America by cultivating the land's abundance and turning the wilderness into a garden. During the Depression, when a return to the Jeffersonian simple life seemed an attractive escape, the farmer persisted as a folk hero; for many, his screen personification was "Hank" Fonda.

Fonda's first film (adapted from his first stage hit) was, appropriately, *The Farmer Takes a Wife*, in which he immediately projected the homespun image that has stayed with him ever since. Tall (6'1") and lanky (but also slightly round-shouldered), he appears to be the essence of what many think of as a rustic type. He possesses a natural grace, exemplified by his distinctive walk, which can only be described as catlike in its delicate deliberateness; as one critic remarked, "He doesn't walk—he flows." His voice has an unmistakable Midwestern drawl, as quiet, as flat and as dry as the plains themselves. And it has been

*LET US LIVE (1939). As Brick Tennant*

As YOUNG MR. LINCOLN (1939)

aid that of all screen actors, Fonda has the most typically American face.

From his debut in 1935 to the end of the thirties, he played a number of farmers and shy, ingenuous boys next door. Even his wealthy characters were often simple, and, despite their refined dress or elegant surroundings, would surely be at ease on the farm. Whether a rustic or not, he conveyed an overwhelming decency, as well as a boyishness and vulnerability (aided by his tendency to whine) that made audiences feel protective. This gave him automatic sympathy as the innocent victim of *You Only Live Once*, one of his major films of the period.

In the late thirties and the forties, he became even more of an archetype with films like *Young Mr. Lincoln*, *The Grapes of Wrath*, *The Ox-Bow Incident*, and *My Darling Clementine*: the rural American who, faced with injustice or lawlessness, accepted as much as possible with stoicism, but began to brood until his slow fuse burned to the inevitable explosion. During this period, Fonda developed to perfection his steady, intense, blue-eyed gaze, which was slightly melancholy, obviously thoughtful, and expressive of a deep concern.

Fonda's decent, concerned hero continued into the fifties, with characters like Mister Roberts and the juror in *12 Angry Men* (his quintessential liberal), and reached a new level in the sixties, when he was the screen's most respected politician (*Advise and Consent*, *The Best Man*, *Fail Safe*). Even in urban settings, or amid the trappings of a complex technological society, he retained the simple virtues of the prairie.

The actor himself is proudest of his socially conscious roles: the films he mentions most often are *The Grapes of Wrath*, *The Ox-Bow Incident* and *12 Angry Men*. But like other stars, he has also enjoyed going against the image. In the forties, his country boy naïveté was the target of humor in *The Lady Eve* and other films, in which Fonda revealed a rich comedic talent. And in recent films, he's had fun playing crooks, villains, and reactionaries.

But with the play *Clarence Darrow* in 1974, he returned to the kind of character that is closest to him: the idealistic, liberal defender of human rights. The image is still that of Midwestern integrity, and what Richard Schickel said in 1962 continues to be valid: "A little bit of what is best about the life of the land clings to his presence."

Fonda has conveyed these qualities through one of the most natural, unpretentious, unmannered acting styles ever to grace

*THE BEST MAN (1964). As William Russell*

the screen. Since his earliest appearances, whether in plays or films, his acting has been described as "effortless," "casual," "underplayed," "understated." To Fonda, the observation that "he doesn't even seem to be acting" is the highest compliment, even if the critic meant it negatively. A perfectionist, he has actually worked extremely hard to give this impression of casualness, to make the audience believe that it is watching a real character, not a performer: "I don't want the wheels to show."

His understated style has often enabled him to merge smoothly into an ensemble, in a completely self-effacing manner, so that even when he's the star he doesn't upstage everyone else; interestingly, this is truest of his three favorite films. Fonda's greatest talent is perhaps as a foil for other, more ostentatious performers, as a reactor rather than an actor, as a man whose face *reflects* much of the drama. This may be the major reason that the Motion Picture Academy, which tends to award histrionics, has seen fit to give him only one nomination in his entire career.

Fonda's restraint is of course essentially cinematic, but of all screen stars he has made the easiest transitions to the stage. For much of his career, he has shuttled from one medium to another; in 1959, in fact, he had a weekly television series, a film in release, and a Broadway role at the same time. Fonda considers himself primarily a stage actor, and has often waited until the last minute to sign for a film, hoping that a script would come along for the new Broadway season.

His disenchantment toward the screen results from the frustration he experiences in not being able to rehearse, in shooting out of sequence, in not building a performance: "You have no recollection of ever creating a character." On stage, he is able to find new subtleties in a character over a period of time: "It just doesn't happen that way in pictures . . . Originally, if we had made a movie instead of a play out of *Roberts*, my performance would have been comparable to the one I gave in the show's out-of-town tryout." Yet he has managed to appear in nearly eighty films; in addition to the enticement of money and an occasional role that he even likes, there's the inescapable realization that it is his reputation as a movie star that draws people to his plays.

Fonda also recognizes his limitations: "I'm not asked—and I shouldn't be asked—to play Shakespeare or Restoration comedy classics today, because I'm still Omaha, Nebraska. I've never tried hard to get away from that. When I have tried, I've felt phony and if I feel phony then it isn't good. I'm Midwest and proud of it . . . . I don't feel I need to apologize to anybody that I'm limited."

He needn't, because this is exactly what has made him a star; all of the screen legends have operated within narrow ranges, to establish images with which the public could easily identify. And, within his range, Fonda has left a body of work unrivalled by that of almost any other actor. Even though he's happy with only a handful of his film roles, there are about two dozen of which he *should* be extremely proud; and his Tom Joad, Abe Lincoln, Wyatt Earp, and Mister Roberts are unquestionably among the screen's immortal characters, with several of his other creations not far behind.

To younger generations, unfortunately, he may be known primarily as the father of Jane and Peter, or, worse, as the man on the GAF commercials. But to anyone who went to the movies from the mid-thirties to the mid-sixties, he was one of the most loved actors, and to many he still has that same box-office appeal. Amazingly, since his first film, he's never been out of work or out of demand; he's been a star for forty years, a feat no other actor can claim. The only other contenders for longevity, James Stewart and John Wayne, actually became stars after he did. Henry Fonda is the most enduring of the screen giants.

# FROM THE FARMLAND TO THE FARMER

The frontier pioneers were an important part of Henry Fonda's heritage. His father's ancestors, descendants of an Italian who had fled to the Netherlands around 1400, had been among the Dutch settlers in New York's Mohawk Valley in the early 1600s. They founded the still-flourishing town of Fonda, in which both of Henry's paternal grandparents were born. The latter, themselves hardy pioneers, left New York and made the long, difficult journey to Nebraska; thus Henry wasn't far removed from the covered wagons and violent frontier settlements so prominent in his films.

Another strong influence was small-town life in the heartland. Henry Jaynes Fonda was born in the prairie city of Grand Island, Nebraska, on May 16, 1905, the first child (there were later two daughters) of Herberta Jaynes and William Brace Fonda. Before Henry was a year old, the family moved to Omaha, where William owned and operated a printing company. Henry had a normal childhood, which included sports, Boy Scouts and the learning of apple-pie morality. Undoubtedly he also heard stories about range wars and conflicts with Indians from old timers, who had been there before the West was won.

Ever since he won a short story contest at the age of ten, he wanted to be a writer, and following his graduation from Omaha Central High School in 1923, he went to the University of Minnesota to study journalism. He worked his way through two years, mostly as director of sports and other activities at a settlement house. Drama played no part in his life, even though a professor once suggested that he take it up. In 1925, at the end of his sophomore year, Fonda, having grown tired of college, quit and returned to Omaha, where he took odd jobs and tried to get newspaper work.

And then he got a call that changed his life. Mrs. Dorothy Brando, a leader of the semi-professional Omaha Community Playhouse (and mother of a one-year-old named Marlon), knew Fonda and thought he was the right age and type for the juvenile lead in Philip Barry's *You and I*. Fonda was shy and had no interest in acting, but she was persuasive, and since he had nothing to do anyway, he agreed. Later Fonda was to say, "If it were not for Mrs. Brando, I would never have become an actor."

The play ran only a week, but he wound up staying at the Playhouse

for the entire nine-month season, painting scenery and finding out what theater was all about. The following summer he had to take a job at a retail credit company, but he managed to work with the Playhouse at night, performing backstage tasks and beginning his addiction to the smell of greasepaint. And early in 1927, he won his first leading role in a one-week run of *Merton of the Movies*. He was a sensation, and even his father, who had disapproved of his growing involvement with the theater, liked his performance. Henry thought it was an exhilarating experience, and he began to think seriously about acting as a profession.

In the spring of 1927 he went to New York, where he saw nine plays in a week; when he returned, he was fully committed to the theater. That summer he wrote a sketch for George Billings, a noted Lincoln impersonator, and included a part for himself. They toured for three months, doing one-night stands in Midwestern cities like Des Moines, where Fonda made his official professional debut. When he returned to the Playhouse for the 1927-28 season, it was as Assistant Director. He designed scenery and even acted opposite Mrs. Brando, but already he was thinking of bigger things. Finally, in June 1928, after three years with the Playhouse, he decided to try his luck in New York, and traveled there with high hopes.

But Broadway was dull during the summer, so he made his way to Cape Cod, seeking to get a job with the legendary Provincetown Players. This proved unsuccessful, but he did become a third assistant stage manager at the Cape Playhouse in Dennis, where Laura Hope Crews and Peggy Wood were working. He also played one lead, and later that summer went to Falmouth, where he took an important step in his career: he joined the University Players, a group of Harvard and Princeton undergraduates who had just formed a summer theater to give students experience before graduation.

It was an extraordinarily talented group of future luminaries, including Bretaigne Windust, Joshua Logan, Kent Smith and Myron McCormick; Margaret Sullavan and Mildred Natwick joined the second year, and a gangly fellow named James Stewart became a member in 1932. Fonda worked with the Players for four years, expanding and enriching his theatrical education. Having never had formal courses in diction, movement, and other dramatic skills, he learned entirely from experience, to which, of course, he added a natural talent. With the Players, he did everything: painting and designing scenery, lighting, making

*On stage with June Walker in THE FARMER TAKES A WIFE (1934)*

off-stage noises, as well as acting in over forty productions and occasionally even directing.

After the summers, when most of the other Players returned to school, Fonda tried New York. From the fall of 1928 until 1934, he struggled for work and recognition. It wasn't easy; parts were ordinarily scarce and the Depression made things worse. But Fonda never became discouraged, even when he had to subsist on rice: "I was damn sure I was a good actor, and sure that eventually I was going to prove it."

He made his Broadway debut in December 1929 in the Theatre Guild's *The Game of Love and Death*, but it was only a bit part as one of the "soldiers and citizens." In the winters of 1928 and 1929, he also worked with the National Junior Theater in Washington, D.C., which performed plays for children. There his main achievement was writing the music and designing the scenery for an original adaptation of *The Wizard of Oz*, which he also directed. And he continued working with the Players. In the winter of 1931, they were performing in Baltimore, where, on Christmas Day, he and his frequent co-star Margaret Sullavan were married. The marriage, unfortunately, was not a success; they fought constantly and about a year later, after she had become a Broadway star, they were divorced.

Fonda left the Players early in 1932 and returned to the Omaha Community Playhouse, where he starred in *A Kiss for Cinderella* with fourteen-year-old Dorothy McGuire. In the summer he worked as handyman and scenic designer, but not actor, at the Surry Playhouse in Maine. There were small roles on Broadway in late 1932 and early 1933, in *I Loved You Wednesday* and *Forsaking All Others*, but in the summer of 1933 he could only get a job as scenic designer again, this time with the Westchester Playhouse in Mount Kisco, New York. He did get to appear in two productions, in which he is said to have stolen the show. He was invited to return the following summer as an actor.

Then, in the spring of 1934, he had his first big break when he did a sketch with Imogene Coca in a Broadway revue, *New Faces of 1934*. Some critics noticed him and called the two a promising comedy team, and as a result of the show Leland Hayward became his agent and manager. Hayward thought Fonda was a natural for the movies, and kept asking him to go to Hollywood to meet producer Walter Wanger. But Fonda, who felt that he was just starting to do well in the theater, wasn't interested. Nevertheless Hayward was persistent, and since Wanger was paying expenses, the actor flew out to Hollywood.

Fonda decided to make his price so high that Wanger wouldn't take him; since he was making $100 a week in New York, he would ask for an exorbitant $350 a week. During a lengthy conference, he kept insisting on staying with the theater, so Wanger guaranteed that he could spend a few months every year on Broadway. Fonda was still about to spring his $350 idea when he heard Wanger offering $1,000 a week. He later said that he was so dazed that he didn't remember having signed the contract.

He still planned to concentrate on the stage, and since no films were ready for him, he returned to Mount Kisco, this time with star billing. One of the plays that summer was *The Swan*, starring Geoffrey Kerr. Kerr's wife, June Walker, saw Fonda and thought him ideal for the lead in *The Farmer Takes a Wife*, which she was scheduled to do on Broadway. Co-author Marc Connelly agreed, and on October 30, 1934, Fonda opened in his first major Broadway role.

A romantic drama about life along the Erie Canal in the 1850s, the play found him in the Mohawk Valley territory of his grandparents. More importantly, it made him a matinee idol and a star. Writing in *The New York Times*, Brooks Atkinson used terms that would recur throughout Fonda's career: "A manly, modest performance in a style of captivating simplicity." The play ran only thirteen weeks, but Fox bought the rights for its leading actress, Janet Gaynor. For the male lead they wanted Gary Cooper or Joel McCrea, but neither was available, and they finally gave the part to Fonda, whom Wanger agreed to loan out.

He arrived in Hollywood in February 1935, three months before his thirtieth birthday. By December he would complete four films; by the end of 1943, he would appear in a total of thirty-four. His dream of being a Broadway star with occasional films would not yet be realized. Whether he liked it or not, Henry Fonda was a movie star.

## PLOWBOYS AND PLAYBOYS

There were no years of struggling in supporting or bit parts, no buildups to stardom. He may have come in through the back door, as a third choice, but Fonda was already a star in his first film. Although in all but one of the eighteen films he made before *Young Mr. Lincoln* he was billed beneath at least one other performer, and although he usually was the foil for someone in a more spectacular part, he never had anything but a major role.

*The Farmer Takes a Wife* (1935) established his image as an unsophisticated, rough-hewn farmer. Dan Harrow works on the Erie Canal, but is interested only in saving up enough money to buy his own land. He falls in love with Molly Larkins (Janet Gaynor), the finest cook on the canal, and persuades her to leave with him for the farm. Deserting the excitement, brawling and intense activity of canal life for the peace of the fields, Dan represents an agrarian individualism that would continue in Fonda's films.

On his first days of shooting, Fonda tended to mug and shout, because he was accustomed to less intimate acting. He credits director Victor Fleming with teaching him how to perform for the camera. The critics were extremely enthusiastic about the boyish actor. *The New York American* said, "Henry Fonda's day dawns.... He dominates the scene and emerges from his film debut a certain film success and one of the really important contributions of stage to screen within the past few seasons." André Sennwald in *The New York Times* remarked, "As the virtuous farm boy he plays with an immensely winning simplicity which will make him one of our most attractive screen actors." His success, however, was touched with sadness: his mother had died in 1934, and his father died shortly before the film's release.

The agrarian image continued in his second film, *Way Down East* (1935), for which Fox again borrowed him from Wanger. Here he plays an upstanding farmer —gentle but sturdy, patient but capable of action—who falls for a hired woman on his father's farm. The father, a self-righteous squire, learns of an affair she had in the past, and turns her out in a blizzard. She winds up floating helplessly down the river on a cake of ice, and Fonda must dash across the ice for a last-minute rescue.

The story, set in Maine in the 1880s, was dated melodrama even as a silent film, but at least the 1920

THE FARMER TAKES A WIFE (1935). With Janet Gaynor

version had D.W. Griffith's direction and Lillian Gish's acting. The remake, directed by the gifted but inferior Henry King, had been intended as another Fonda-Gaynor vehicle, but Gaynor, who might have helped, had to drop out because of illness, and she was replaced by bland Rochelle Hudson.

Before taking on another bucolic role in *The Trail of the Lonesome Pine*, Fonda appeared in the first of his more "sophisticated" parts, in RKO's *I Dream Too Much* (1935).

The film, a vehicle for opera star Lily Pons' screen debut, has Fonda as an amiable American who longs to be a respected opera composer. He marries a provincial Frenchwoman (Pons), who rises to success as an opera star while he remains a failure. They separate, but all ends well when she gets his opera performed as a musical comedy, puts it over herself, and prepares to be a mother.

As in many other films, Fonda's personality must defer to that of his more histrionic co-star: Pons often takes over the spotlight, singing grand opera as well as musical numbers by Jerome Kern and Dorothy Fields. But at times both performers are upstaged by "The Duchess," a trained seal owned by their delightfully eccentric neighbor (Eric Blore).

Wanger had loaned Fonda out three times before finding a film for him. Finally, he cast the actor in *The Trail of the Lonesome Pine* (1936). The story, which had been filmed twice in the silent era, deals with a generations-old feud between two Kentucky mountain families. Dave Tolliver (Fonda), one of the most militant feuders, also dislikes a city slicker (Fred MacMurray), who's building a railroad on their land, and who convinces Dave's girl (Sylvia Sidney) to leave the mountains and become educated. Dave eventually overcomes his hatreds and sacrifices his life to end the feud.

Dave possesses a number of traits found in subsequent Fonda characters: he is brooding, sullen and often violent, yet capable of tenderness; he dislikes running from a fight; and he's opposed to "progress." He speaks disparagingly of civilization, represented by machines and the railroad (the latter a recurring symbol of the evils of progress), and, anticipating Muley's speech in *The Grapes of Wrath* and his own in *Blockade*, he says he was

*WAY DOWN EAST (1935). With Rochelle Hudson*

*I DREAM TOO MUCH (1935). With Lily Pons and Billy Gilbert*

born in the soil and will die in it.

Fonda's expressively restrained performance was overshadowed not only by Sidney's more fiery acting, but by the fact that this was the first outdoor feature in three-color Technicolor. Director Henry Hathaway subdued the colors, avoiding the extravagant stylization of *Becky Sharp*, the first feature in the process, released a year earlier; with its warm browns and greens, and hazy blue mountains, it is breathtakingly lovely even today. (One person who did notice Fonda, incidentally, was Al Capp, who claimed that Dave Tolliver was his inspiration for Li'l Abner.)

Fonda's next two films, both for Wanger, returned him to comedy. He was teamed with Margaret Sullavan in his first screwball comedy, *The Moon's Our Home* (1936). There was speculation that they would remarry once her divorce from William Wyler became final, but instead she married Leland Hayward, who was both Fonda's and Wyler's agent.

The film itself concerns a tempestuous marriage. A temperamental Hollywood actress and a successful travel writer dislike each other by reputation, but haven't met. Traveling incognito to escape their fans (appropriately, he pretends he's a farm boy), they meet, and, still preserving their identities from each other, get married. There are many misunderstandings, quarrels, and reunions; particularly amusing is their violent argument during the wedding ceremony, in which their coincidental screams of "I do!" are mistaken by the deaf justice of the peace to be marriage vows. Fonda is engaging, although again his co-star—permitted to indulge in explosive tantrums in which she throws everything in sight—has the more glamorous role.

In *Spendthrift* (1936), another romantic comedy, Fonda is a millionaire playboy who's spent his entire $23,000,000, a fact he comprehends only with great difficulty. However, he determines to make an honest living, and gets a job as a radio announcer at $1,000 a week. After some misadventures with a gold digger (Mary Brian), he finds his true (proletarian) love—a stableman's daughter (Pat Paterson).

Like other Depression movies, this one puts the idle rich through punishment, but by 1936 the partial return to prosperity apparently meant that movies could be easier on millionaires: $1,000 a week was sufficient hardship, and at least he had to work for it. In any event, this was a minor film for both Fonda and director Raoul Walsh.

Fonda next traveled to the British Isles on loan-out to 20th Century-Fox, for Britain's first three-color Technicolor feature, *Wings of the Morning* (1937). As with *The Trail of the Lonesome*

THE TRAIL OF THE LONESOME PINE (1936). With Sylvia Sidney and Beulah Bondi

THE MOON'S OUR HOME (1936). With Margaret Sullavan

*Pine*, the critics paid more attention to the color than to anything else, but the film's plot is negligible anyway.

French actress Annabella, in her first English-speaking role, is a Spanish duchess who flees the Spanish Civil War disguised as a boy. In Ireland she falls in love with a Canadian horse-trainer (Fonda). For no logical reason, she remains in disguise, which occasions some humorous scenes, as when she attends him in his bath, spends the night with him in a hayloft, and refuses to take off her trousers.

While in London, Fonda met Frances Seymour Brokaw, a widow and mother of a five-year-old girl. They were married in New York on September 16, 1936. The combination of Homespun Hank and the worldly twenty-eight-year-old socialite was the topic of much Hollywood skepticism, but it seemed that Fonda was settling into a happy marriage.

His career was also taking a fortunate turn. A few days after his wedding, Fonda was hard at work on Wanger's *You Only Live Once* (1937), which stands far above all of his other films up to *Young Mr. Lincoln*. Fritz Lang's second American film (after his acclaimed *Fury*), it is one of the masterpieces of the thirties, and it established another image for Fonda: the man falsely accused of a crime and trapped in an inescapable web of circumstance. Hitchcock would use this twenty years later in *The Wrong Man*.

Eddie Taylor (Fonda) isn't a complete innocent: he's been in reform schools, has served three prison terms for robbery, and knows that another conviction will mean life imprisonment. But he wants desperately to go straight; he starts on a job, and he and his bride, Joan (Sylvia Sidney), plan to buy a house and settle down. Their hopes are destroyed when he's convicted of murder and robbery on the basis of circumstantial evidence and is sentenced to death. He stages a prison break, during which a pardon comes through. Thinking it's a trick, he shoots the chaplain in confusion. He and Joan flee across the country, stealing only to eat, but blamed for robberies they didn't commit. The police hunt them down and brutally kill them.

This was the first of many films inspired by the story of Bonnie and Clyde, but Lang's characters (unlike Arthur Penn's, for example) are not glamorous, willful criminals; they are totally victimized by a cruel society that will not let them lead normal lives. Eddie is innocent but is forced by society to become a murderer.

But Lang isn't a social critic, hoping the world can change; he's a pessimist who believes that people are at the mercy of a cold, implacable

*SPENDTHRIFT (1936). With Pat Paterson, Edward Brophy, and J.M. Kerrigan*

fate, and he's fascinated with how they combat their destinies. As Peter Bogdanovich says, Eddie "is as doomed from the start as Oedipus; but for Lang, it is not the outcome that matters in a struggle against fate, it is the fight itself."* Lang likes to place characters in hopeless situations and observe them as they try to escape; Eddie and Joan, like the murderer in *M*, are typical of the trapped creatures of Lang's nightmare world. This terrifying vision is reinforced by his expressionistic style: dramatic lighting, foreboding angles, tracking shots imprisoning characters, scenes shrouded in fog, images of entrapment.

Fonda gives a masterful performance. His soft speech and sincere manner initially convince us of his desire for normalcy. But there's already a slight insecurity, a vulnerability, an awareness that the world is unstable. His edginess and controlled hostility finally erupt into violence when he hits the man who's fired him. He then becomes bitter and hard—screaming his innocence at the crowds who mob him, looking mean and furtive as he asks Joan to bring a gun to the jail, speaking in angry, intense whispers during the escape. His bitterness combines with a continual look of bewilderment, suiting Lang's con-

---

*Peter Bogdanovich, *Fritz Lang in America*, Praeger, 1969, p. 8

ception of a man both angry and helpless in the face of the whims of destiny.

According to Bogdanovich, Lang is one of the cinema's greatest creators of nightmares; according to Fonda, the film itself was "a tortured nightmare to make." At the time, he complained that Lang pinched actors to get reactions and treated them like puppets. In recent interviews, Fonda has repeatedly told how infuriated he was at watching Lang spend hours setting up shots: "I hate Fritz Lang... he was too preoccupied with what everything was going to look like." Paradoxically, Fonda, who is known as a perfectionist, disliked Lang primarily for his meticulous attention to detail.

From the high point of *You Only Live Once*, Fonda descended somewhat to Warners' pleasant but routine programmer, *Slim* (1937). Here again he is a farm boy, but one who *hates* plows, and who determines to be a lineman after he sees a group of them stringing high voltage wires across his farm. A veteran lineman, Red (Pat O'Brien), gets Slim a job, and teaches him the hazardous work. He also tries to keep the young man out of trouble, but both love brawling; at one point Slim gets stabbed while helping

*WINGS OF THE MORNING (1937). With Annabella*

*YOU ONLY LIVE ONCE (1937). With Sylvia Sidney*

*YOU ONLY LIVE ONCE (1937). With Guinn Williams*

Red in a fight. (Here, as in later films, Fonda rushes to the aid of others.)

Through documentary-like scenes of the linework, the film celebrates the men's courage. As in most action films, women only get in the way. Red's girl (Margaret Lindsay), whom he won't marry because that would tie him down, falls for Slim, and almost convinces him to quit. But when Red falls to his death as they work on cables during a snowstorm, Slim faces her resolutely and says he must finish the job. Despite his own injury sustained in trying to save Red, he climbs back up. Like Young Mr. Lincoln, he is last seen as an heroic figure, moving onward to face his destiny.

Still on loan to Warners, he appeared in *That Certain Woman* (1937), as a rich playboy who marries the widow (Bette Davis) of a murdered gangster. His prominent

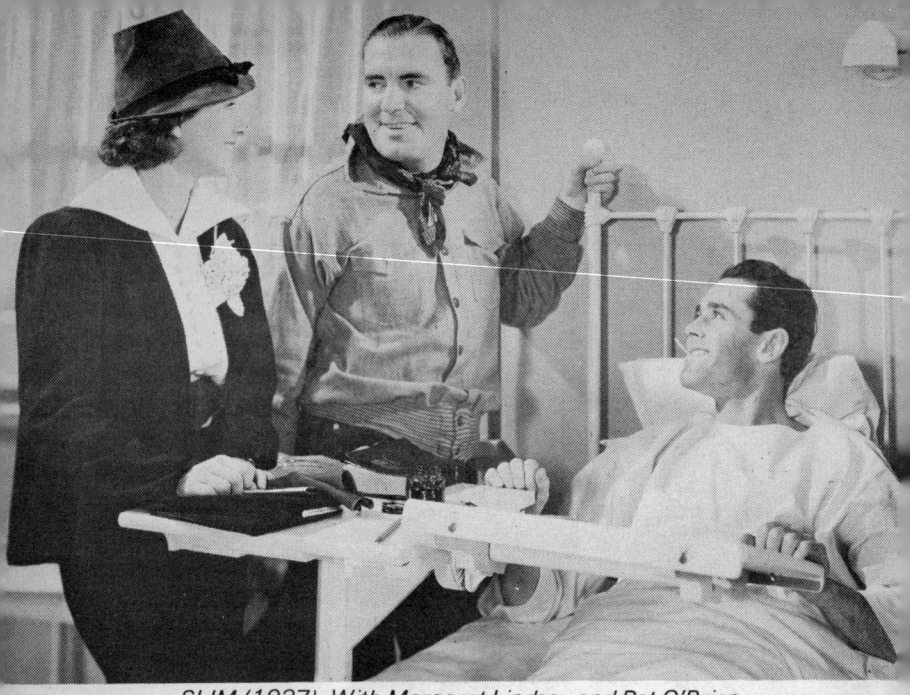

*SLIM (1937). With Margaret Lindsay and Pat O'Brien*

father (Donald Crisp) disapproves of the former moll and has the marriage annulled, whereupon Fonda, not realizing that Davis is pregnant, leaves for Europe and weds his childhood sweetheart (Anita Louise). Four years later he returns and finds out about the child. His wife, now crippled, offers him to Davis who, in an equally self-sacrificing mood, refuses to hurt the other woman. Luckily, Louise dies, leaving Davis and Fonda free to reunite.

Edmund Goulding wrote and directed this absurd tear-jerker, a remake of his own *The Trespasser* (1929), Gloria Swanson's first talkie.

Fonda seems uncomfortable throughout. One minor irony, considering his farmer roles, is his assurance to Davis that he can work as well as anyone: "I may not have done much work behind a plow, but . . ."

These loan-out assignments weren't very satisfying, but Fonda was equally unlucky when he returned to Wanger for *I Met My Love Again* (1938). Here the male-female roles of *That Certain Woman* are reversed: Fonda is jilted by his impetuous sweetheart (Joan Bennett), who prefers the Bohemian life in Paris. He becomes a staid, embittered college professor. Ten years later, she returns, a widow with a grown daughter. He must decide whether or not to reunite with her—a decision complicated by a student's threat to commit suicide unless he marries *her*. The film was inconsequential, but it did enable Fonda to work with his old friend, Joshua Logan, who co-directed with Arthur Ripley.

Fonda's ping-pong movements brought him back to Warners, where he was again teamed with Bette Davis in a tear-jerker. *Jezebel* (1938), like *That Certain Woman*, is really Davis' vehicle. Reportedly she had turned down *Gone with the Wind* because she didn't want to co-star in it with Errol Flynn (David O. Selznick's early choice for Rhett Butler), and as a consolation, Warners gave her *Jezebel*, another drama about a temperamental Southern belle. (Fonda, coincidentally, in 1936 had expressed a desire to do *Gone with the Wind*.)

The setting is New Orleans in 1852. Preston Dillard (Fonda), an upright banker, is engaged to Julie Morrison (Davis), a spoiled, wealthy, extremely independent coquette who, out of spite, tries to embarrass him by wearing a red dress to a ball where all proper unmarried ladies wear virginal white. Tired of her perverse flouting of convention, Pres leaves her, but she, like the heroine in *That Certain Woman*, is certain that he'll come back.

*THAT CERTAIN WOMAN (1937). With Bette Davis*

*I MET MY LOVE AGAIN (1938). With Joan Bennett*

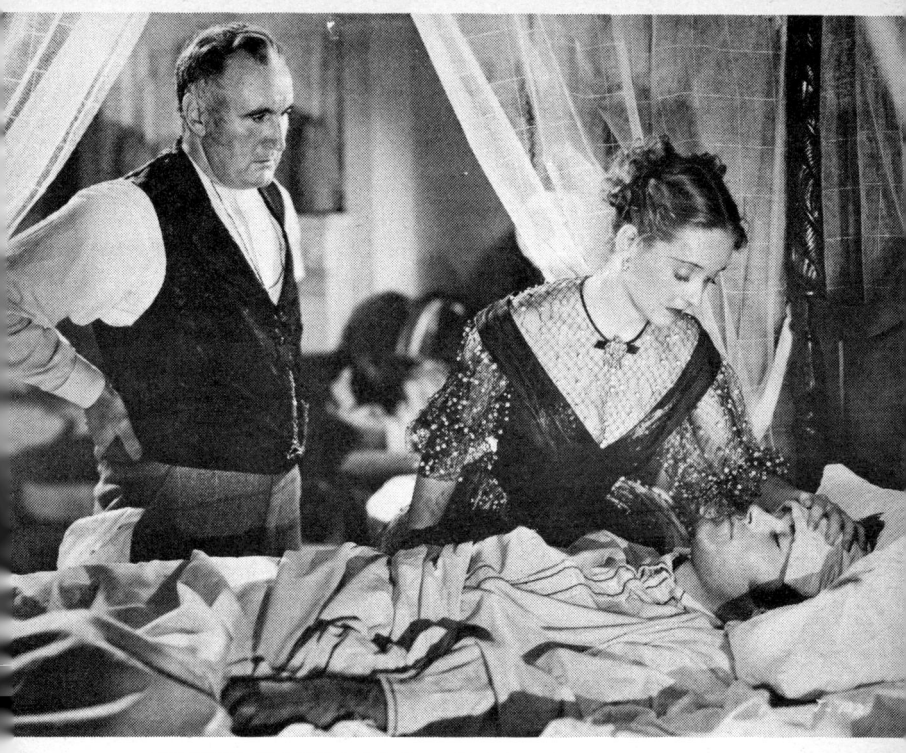

*JEZEBEL (1938). With Donald Crisp and Bette Davis*

As in the Goulding film, he returns, married to a gentle woman. Julie's revenge leads to the death of her former suitor (George Brent) in a senseless duel, but Julie gets a chance to repent for her recklessness. When Pres is stricken with yellow fever, she bravely volunteers to nurse him back to health on a disease-ridden island; in another battle of self-sacrifice, she wins over the weaker wife.

It's soap opera, but directed by William Wyler in a glossy, entertaining manner. And Davis, moving smoothly through a wide range of moods—she's obstinate, brooding, vivacious, imperious, teasing, contrite—has rarely been better. (She won an Oscar.) Fonda's role, which is far less complex, calls for him to be rather stiff for much of the film.

But there are effective moments: the scene in which he pleads, then screams angrily, when Julie locks him out of her room; the argument with the other men, in which he sadly predicts that their way of life is doomed; the ball, where he returns all of the stares with a belligerent look, then forces Julie—who has succeeded only in embarrassing herself—to keep dancing, while the others, outraged, desert the floor.

One sidelight to *Jezebel:* during the filming, Fonda had to leave for New York where, on December 21, 1937, his wife gave birth to their first child, Jane Seymour Fonda.

The actor expanded upon his previous agrarian characterizations in his next film, Wanger's *Blockade* (1938), a controversial drama about the then-raging Spanish Civil War. Here the farmer becomes an eloquent defender of his land—a Spanish peasant who passionately loves the soil and whose purpose in fighting is to prevent the enemy from taking it over.

The film is flawed by its unwillingness to identify the opposing sides; at no time, in fact, does there seem to be a *civil* war—the enemy is more like a foreign invader. But a much more unfortunate compromise was the introduction of a conventional romance and spy story. Fonda becomes involved with a beautiful woman (Madeleine Carroll), who turns out to be an enemy agent, but who eventually has a change of heart. Scenarist John Howard Lawson, admitting that this spoiled the film, states simply: "The artifice was required in order to give the film a commercial gloss."

Still, considering Hollywood's

*BLOCKADE (1938). With Madeleine Carroll*

*SPAWN OF THE NORTH (1938). With Dorothy Lamour, Lynne Overman, Louise Platt, George Raft, and John Barrymore*

traditional avoidance of sensitive political issues, *Blockade* was fairly bold. William Dieterle directed the scenes of the struggling masses with conviction (and with some large borrowings from *Potemkin*), and apparently enough people did recognize the enemy as Franco, because the Catholic Church attacked the film, and several cities banned it.

As in previous films such as *Slim*, Fonda is appealing as the shy lover. His underplaying contrasts pleasingly with Carroll's hysterics, and his already evident look of concern is effective. He's also convincing in two highly emotional scenes. As his fellow villagers flee the enemy, he manages to halt the retreat. Standing on an embankment, his voice breaking with excitement, he cries: "Stop—turn back! . . . This valley —it's ours—it's part of us. We were born here—our fathers were, and their fathers before them . . . turn back and fight!"

And, at the end, foreshadowing Joel McCrea's final scene in Wanger's 1940 film, *Foreign Correspondent*, he looks at us and pleads for help: "It's murder—murder of innocent people. There's no sense to it. The world can stop it. Where's the conscience of the world?" Unfortunately the speech loses much of its force because the issues are so muddled. Fonda himself feels that the character didn't ring true, because as a farmer he had to speak lines appropriate to an Oxford graduate.

In Paramount's *Spawn of the North* (1938), Fonda isn't a farmer,

*THE MAD MISS MANTON (1938). With Barbara Stanwyck and Sam Levene*

but he's still a rugged frontier type. The frontier here is Alaska, where honest fishermen Fonda and George Raft battle Russian pirates. Their friendship is tested when Raft joins the pirates, but he proves that he's honorable after all. Fonda is paired with Louise Platt in a romance, but the emphasis is on epic outdoor adventure, at which Henry Hathaway (*The Trail of the Lonesome Pine*) is expert. The film has some brisk action scenes, as well as the invigorating presence of John Barrymore as a garrulous newspaper editor appropriately named "Windy."

RKO's *The Mad Miss Manton* (1938), an amusing screwball comedy-mystery in the *Thin Man* tradition, was a considerable change of pace. Fonda plays a newsman who ridicules a group of nutty debutantes when they claim they've discovered a murder. He thinks it's merely another gag played by the idle rich, especially since the corpse has vanished. The seven women, led by daffy heiress Barbara Stanwyck, set out to prove him wrong and solve the murder. Along the way they find additional corpses, and naturally there's a romance between Fonda and Stanwyck.

On this, the first of three films

they made together, Fonda and his co-star did not get along. But things improved three years later, when they did *The Lady Eve*, and recently Fonda said, "My all-time favorite was Stanwyck... the most loved person ever to walk on a movie set. Nothing phony in her real life or on screen."

Fonda kept returning to the farm, and in his first Western, Fox's *Jesse James* (1939), he was once again fighting (as in *Blockade*) to keep his land. Here the enemy is the railroad (which the opening titles call an "ogre"), forcing people from their farms and offering little compensation. The James family, like the Joads in *The Grapes of Wrath*, are honest, clean-living folks caught up in the destructive tide of "civilization." When Jesse (Tyrone Power) and Frank (Fonda) resist, their mother is accidentally killed by thugs hired to oust the family from their home, and they set out on a bitter road of vengeance.

The film therefore justifies their actions, which are mostly taken against the railroad, and it even ends with the unveiling of a monument to Jesse. Like many other Westerns, it reveals an ambivalence toward the opening of the frontier: a sense of epic discovery and excitement, mingled with a feeling that with each step in westward expansion, something was lost—most im-

*JESSE JAMES (1939). With (in foreground) Tyrone Power, Henry Hull, and Jane Darwell*

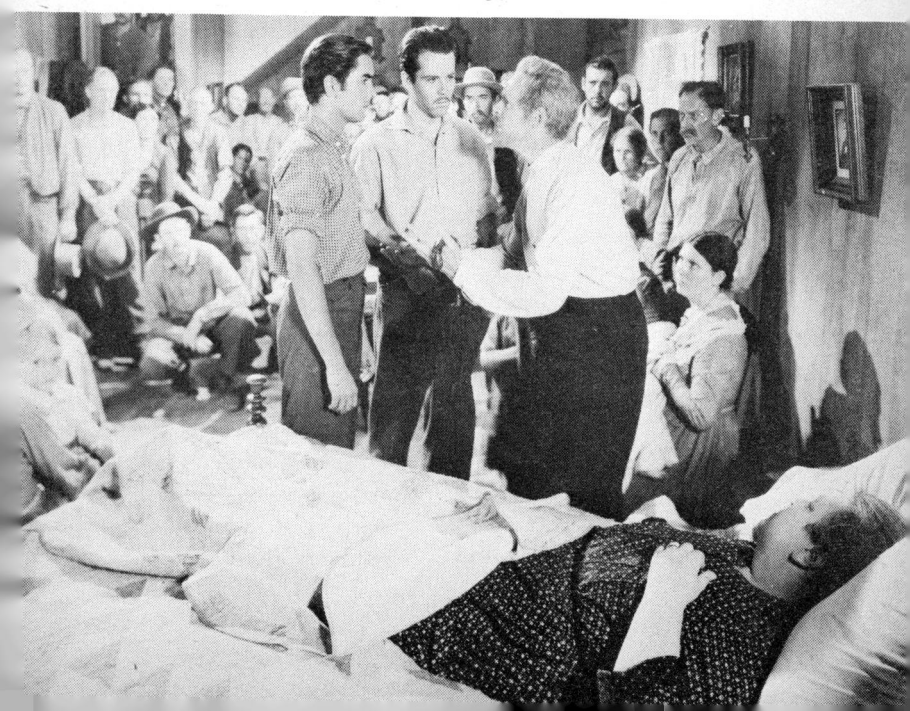

*LET US LIVE (1939). Brick Tennant is arrested.*

portantly, the simple life of the upright, individual frontier farmer.

Tyrone Power, Fox's leading actor, was naturally selected for the lead, and his character—attractive, daring, roguish—is more flamboyant than Fonda's. Unlike Jesse, Frank is quiet, calm, self-possessed and nonchalant when facing his enemies, and Fonda—chewing tobacco and underplaying throughout—steals the film. During the train holdup, he is charming and gentlemanly, thanking the passengers and reminding them to sue the railroad. His best scene is the one in which he calms his headstrong "kid brother" with a combination of love and quiet forcefulness. The film itself is a lively Western, distinguished by director Henry King's subdued use of Technicolor.

While *Jesse James* added dimension to one Fonda image Columbia's *Let Us Live* (1939 merely reiterated another. The film is, in fact, virtually a remake of *You Only Live Once*, but, as often happened in the days before television and revival houses showed ol movies, few critics noticed th similarities. Even more than Lang film, it is a forerunner c Hitchcock's *The Wrong Man* Fonda plays a poor but ambitiou cab driver who is about to marry waitress (Maureen O'Sullivan) when he and his roommate are mis takenly identified as the men wh robbed a theater and committe murder. Circumstantial evidenc convicts them, and O'Sullivan' desperate attempts to save Fonda are futile until a detective (Ralph Bellamy) finally believes her.

Like Hitchcock's film, it was based on a news story, although in actuality the real criminals were caught while the wrong men were still on trial, whereas the film increases the suspense by waiting until just before the execution. It ends grimly, with Fonda a bitter man; as in Lang's work, he is hardened by society's injustices. The entire film is somber, and is directed in intense expressionist style by another German expatriate, John Brahm. But it's a rather pale imitation of *You Only Live Once*.

The first phase of Fonda's movie career was nearing an end. Although it had established the basic characteristics of his persona, it had also seen him hopping among studios and directors, and from one genre to another, frequently with less than spectacular results. The final film of this period, *The Story of Alexander Graham Bell* (1939), was characteristic. Like *Young Mr. Lincoln*, his next film, it was the kind of expensive historical biography for which Darryl F. Zanuck and 20th Century-Fox had become famous. But here Fonda had merely a secondary role: he played Thomas Watson, Bell's sensible though not

*THE STORY OF ALEXANDER GRAHAM BELL (1939).* With Don Ameche

brilliant assistant, and supported Don Ameche, as he had recently supported Zanuck's other leading actor, Tyrone Power, in *Jesse James*.

In an otherwise dull, reverential film, Fonda does provide some welcome comic relief with his laconic sarcasm. And his dazed reaction —"It talked!" —to the first phone transmission, with his voice breaking like an adolescent's, is the film's highlight. Nonetheless, it was hardly a memorable performance; everyone knows that Don Ameche invented the telephone, but who recalls that when he said, "Mr. Watson, come here, I need you," he was summoning Henry Fonda?

The film indicates the rut into which he had fallen, and from which he was pulled by John Ford. *Young Mr. Lincoln* was released just two months later, but it was a gigantic leap in his career.

Fonda had appeared in eighteen films when Darryl F. Zanuck asked him to star in Fox's *Young Mr. Lincoln*. He turned down the role, saying, "Lincoln's too big a man. Not only too big in history, but too big in everyone's heart and affections. I'm not ready for a part like that." But Zanuck and director John Ford explained that instead of the great Lincoln, this would be the young man in whom greatness could be faintly glimpsed. Fonda accepted, beginning an alliance with Ford that changed his career. Ford enlarged upon the actor's previous qualities, giving them greater significance and creating a group of archetypal representatives of decency, conscience, courage, tradition, and the American character.

There was an immediate sympathy between Fonda and Ford. As Lindsay Anderson has said, "If one examines the personality of the actor, one finds it clearly complementary to that of the director, as each reveals himself in his best work. In Fonda as in Ford, there is the same rare combination of sensibility with authority, gentleness with strength; the same openness of feeling; the same compulsive integrity that reveals itself with a directness so seemingly simple that it is easy to overlook the artistry that such revelation, such simplicity, demand."*

# MR. FONDA AND MR. FORD

By the time he made *Lincoln* in 1939, Ford had already directed about ninety films, including the widely praised *The Informer* (1935), but *Lincoln* may be his first masterpiece. While *The Informer* seems self-conscious and artificial today, *Lincoln* endures as a piece of artfully simple screen poetry—a perfectly realized combination of realism and nostalgia, tenderness and humor, historical significance and intimate personal drama. It is perhaps Fonda's greatest film, one that gave him an opportunity to explore a wide range of his acting abilities, and to create his first immortal screen character. If *The Farmer Takes a Wife* made him a star, *Lincoln* decisively made him an actor.

Ford and scenarist Lamar Trotti depict Lincoln between the ages of twenty-three and thirty: his initial involvement with politics in 1832; his tragic romance with Ann Rutledge; his first law practice in Springfield in 1837; his early acquaintance with Mary Todd and

* Lindsay Anderson, "John Ford," *Cinema*, Spring, 1971, p. 34.

*YOUNG MR. LINCOLN (1939). With Pauline Moore*

Stephen Douglas; his defense of two brothers unjustly accused of murder. These are set against an evocative panorama of early Midwestern America, when political campaigns were on the town-meeting level, law questions could be settled by the *Farmer's Almanac*, feelings of friendship, family, and community (qualities Ford always admires) prevailed, and the nation was still in its awkward but wonderfully innocent infancy.

Fonda miraculously evokes Lincoln's appearance. Of course he already had the appropriate lankiness and height (like Lincoln, he's 6' ", although he increased this height with elevator shoes), and the makeup artists added a false nose, a mole, the illusion of deeply set eyes and a protruding brow. But this would be just a stunt if Fonda did not also convey—through his posture, gestures and speech—what people felt was the essence of Lincoln's personality. He succeeds where most other actors portraying great people have failed: in imparting greatness and dignity without ever being pompous, stilted, or self-consciously important. We relate to Lincoln as a believable human being, not as an awesome giant of history.

The actor draws on his previous characterizations, but there's no precedent in his career for such a fully rounded portrait; he's at once awkward and eloquent, simple and shrewd, humble and courageous, brooding and amiable, melancholy and witty. One remembers his modest first speech, in which he calls himself "plain Abraham Lincoln"; his folksy way of settling legal disputes; his clumsy, gangly gestures and seeming inability to find a place for his long legs (he usually ends up reclining, with his feet up); his stiffness in dancing with Mary; the climactic trial, in which he upstages and subtly ridicules the prosecutor with his dry, homespun humor, but is also intense and thoughtful when necessary.

Ford's poetic simplicity is evident in his condensing the Lincoln-Rutledge relationship into a single haunting scene. The two walk alongside a river, talking about his career plans. When he tells her she's pretty, she says some folks don't like red hair. He replies, "I do—I love red hair." They look at each other, and she continues walking. That's all we need to know: the deeper emotion remains unspoken. He throws a stone into the river, and Ford dissolves to winter, with ice now flowing and Lincoln sadly trudging to her gravesite. Fonda is poignantly expressive as he looks at Ann's grave and confides his confusion about whether to enter the law. Later, when he's with Mary, he suddenly becomes transfixed by the sight of a river, conveying through a

*YOUNG MR. LINCOLN (1939). With Ward Bond*

simple gaze the memory of a lost love.

There are also more melodramatic scenes, such as his confrontation with a lynch mob who are after the two young brothers. Breaking through the crowd, he stands in front of them, complaining that they're trying to do him out of his first clients, and assuring them that with him handling the case they'll have nothing to worry about: his down-to-earth, homey manner is that of a man gently chastising some friends. He also remarks, "We seem to lose our heads in times like this. We do things together that we'd be mighty ashamed to do by ourselves." This simple prairie lawyer is the prototype for Fonda's idealistic, determined defenders of the innocent.

Ford reserves his full expression of Lincoln as the man of destiny for the last scene. After the boys have been acquitted, and Lincoln says good-bye to their departing family, he decides not to go back home right away: "I think I might go on a piece—maybe to the top of that hill." As he walks toward the horizon and a dramatic thunderstorm begins, he becomes both the humble Lincoln we have seen and the grand figure moving on to glory. It's a powerful example of what Andrew Sarris has said about Ford's style: "A double vision of an event in all its vital immediacy and yet also in its ultimate memory image on the horizon of history."*

Ford and Fonda, who both re-

*Andrew Sarris, *The American Cinema*, E.P. Dutton, 1968, p. 48

*DRUMS ALONG THE MOHAWK (1939). As Gilbert Martin*

ceived almost unanimous critical acclaim for *Lincoln*, reunited immediately for Fox's *Drums Along the Mohawk* (1939), Ford's first color film and another critical success. Like *The Farmer Takes a Wife*, it was based on a Walter Edmonds novel, with Fonda again a simple farmer from the Mohawk Valley who takes a bride back to his farm, this time during the Revolutionary War. Lana (Claudette Colbert), a cultured Albany belle, is accustomed to comfort and luxury, and has difficulty adjusting to life in a log cabin. Gradually, however, she develops a taste for clearing the land and farming, and her pioneer spirit equals that of her husband, Gil. They survive hardships, her miscarriage, and attacks by savage Indians (who, goaded by Tories, destroy their farm and the surrounding community) to see the end of the war.

This is one of Ford's most stirring tributes to pioneer courage—to people who manage to preserve love, comradeship and family, and who become ennobled through struggle. Despite immense obstacles, a nation is born, which Ford indicates through his recurring symbols of civilization, community and continuity: the group's shared excitement when Lana finally gives birth; the combined effort to clear the land and rebuild the settlement; the pioneers' dance.

The emphasis is on the maintenance of tradition; at no time are we aware that this is a rebellion, and the word "British" is never even mentioned. Of course this is due somewhat to the world situation in 1939, when the British were themselves threatened, and when the struggle against evil invaders had more meaning than did revolution. But it is also part of the personal mythology of Ford (conservative rather than radical) and Fonda (the farmer protecting his land from outsiders' trespassing). When the coonskin-capped rabble are formed into a local militia, the general tells them that they are defending their homes and land, that Congress cannot help them with regular troops so "the frontier will have to look out for itself." The determination of individuals, not the government, will defeat the enemies.

In the final scene, the war has ended and—amid the activity of rebuilding the fort—the American flag is raised (significantly, on another symbol of civilization, the church) for the first time. As "America" is heard on the sound track, and the settlers stare at the flag, Gil turns to Lana and says, "Well, I reckon we'd better be gettin' back to work. There's gonna be a heap to do from now on." It is admittedly sentimental and flag-waving, but also poetic and moving, as Ford's archetypal American pre-

*DRUMS ALONG THE MOHAWK (1939). With Claudette Colbert*

pares for the task of building the country.

Even more affecting is a scene —one of Fonda's best ever—in which Gil has returned from a massacre, and is propped up against a wall while his wounds are treated. In an extraordinary three-minute take, Fonda, staring ahead numbly and speaking in a mumbling, halting manner, tells of seeing men dying, and of having to put one of them out of his misery. Echoing earlier Fonda characters, but with the added significance of a crucial moment in our history, he ends with, "But we won—we licked them—we showed them they couldn't take this valley."

In Ford's (as well as Fonda's) next

*THE GRAPES OF WRATH (1940). With Jane Darwell, Dorris Bowdon, Shirley Mills, Russell Simpson, Frank Darien, and Joseph Sawyer*

*THE GRAPES OF WRATH (1940). With Russell Simpson and Frank Darien*

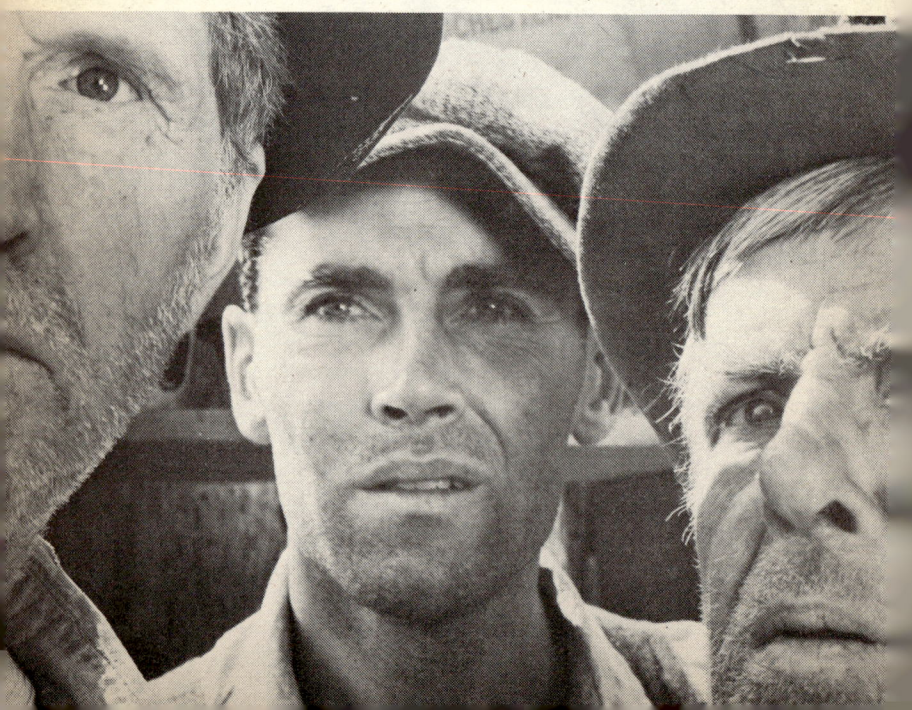

film, *The Grapes of Wrath* (1940), the Oklahoma Dust Bowl farmers ("Okies") are depicted as fighting a similar battle. Although here the invader—the impersonal bank—succeeds in evicting the Joads from their farm, they retain their agrarian dignity on their courageous but hopeless odyssey to the elusive promised land. Unlike Steinbeck, who portrayed them as wretched representatives of an oppressed mass, Ford sees them as an heroic, isolated unit. As before, Ford's concern is with the small group or family threatened by destruction and ennobled by their determination to remain together and survive.

Steinbeck suggested that the masses' anger will make them unite to solve their problems, whereas Ford and scriptwriter Nunnally Johnson offer a less militant solution. At the end, Ma (Jane Darwell) says that despite their beating, the people will go on forever. The idea is to persist and hope for the best, instead of trying to change society: to find strength in tradition and continuity. In this light, the decision by Tom (Fonda) to take social action is a highly individual, and probably not very viable approach. He's one of only a handful of rebellious men in the film, and the others are either defeated or killed.

Still, Ford makes us feel Tom's anger and shows it as an understandable result of continual humiliation. Fonda was a perfect choice for the role: the essence of rural decency, with the intense gaze of a man deep in thought and on the verge of exploding. In *Jesse James*, he defended his rights against the railroad, and though the tractor is the new mechanical monster here, the conflict is the same.

At first, released from prison to which he was sent for homicide, he's surly and sullen, with a general resentment similar to Eddie's in *You Only Live Once*. Upon learning that his family has been uprooted, he is bewildered, but becomes more focused in his anger. And as they experience antagonism and disappointment in one migrant camp after another, he grows increasingly bitter. Finally he takes direct action, standing up for innocent people by striking back and killing the man who's murdered Casy, the preacher (John Carradine).

There are also pleasanter moments in the film. One of Fonda's best scenes is his talk with the FDR-like director of the government camp, whose kindness and democratic approach are a welcome relief. (Ford sees New Deal benevolence as an acceptable answer.) Incredulous and restrained in his delight for fear that it's too good to be true, Tom smiles shyly and says, "Ma's sure gonna like it here—she ain't been treated decent in a long while." At the camp's dance (again, a sure sign of civilization) he whirls around the floor with Ma, laughs for the only time in the film, and even sings a bit of "Red River Valley."

But the emphasis is on his growing determination to act, culminating in his speech to Ma in the darkness, as he leaves to find out the reasons for social injustice. Although the speech is incongruous for this rather inarticulate man, and less radical in its context than in the novel's, it is memorable for Fonda's sincere delivery. Ma, realizing that this may be their last time together, asks how she'll know what is happening to him. Staring straight ahead, with his earnest, concerned look, he replies that perhaps Casy was right—that each soul is just a piece of "the one big soul," the soul of mankind:

"Then it don't matter. I'll be all aroun' in the dark. I'll be everywhere—wherever you can look. Wherever there's a fight so hungry people can eat, I'll be there. Wherever there's a cop beatin' up a guy, I'll be there. I'll be in the way guys yell when they're mad—an' I'll be in the way kids laugh when they're hungry an' they know supper is ready. An' when the people are eatin' the stuff they raise, an' livin' in the houses they build, I'll be there too."

This speech alone probably made Tom Joad a legendary screen hero; certainly it was the role most associated with Fonda for years, and it influenced the nature of his subsequent socially conscious characters. The film itself, of course, is considered a classic: its gallery of vivid portraits, mood of poignant nostal-

THE GRAPES OF WRATH (1940). With Dorris Bowdon and Jane Darwell

*MY DARLING CLEMENTINE (1946). With Cathy Downs*

gia, stunning photography by Gregg Toland, and courage in dealing with a contemporary issue make it almost as powerful today as in 1940, when it was a huge critical and commercial success. It was nominated for seven Academy Awards, with both Ford and Darwell winning. But the film itself lost to Hitchcock's *Rebecca*, and Fonda, nominated for the only time in his career, lost to his friend James Stewart (*The Philadelphia Story*). It is said that Stewart won because he had lost the previous year, when he was up for *Mr. Smith Goes to Washington*.

One of the film's admirers was John Steinbeck, who became Fonda's lifelong friend, and believed that the actor embodied what he stood for. Fonda narrated two television adaptations of Steinbeck, *America and Americans* and *Travels with Charley*, and appeared in a television movie of *The Red Pony* (1973). The author's last appearance was at a 1968 dinner honoring

Fonda, and the actor eulogized Steinbeck at his funeral later that year.

To appear in *The Grapes of Wrath*, Fonda had to sacrifice his freedom, which he had won when his contract with Wanger had expired. Zanuck had originally wanted Tyrone Power or Don Ameche(!), who were both under contract to him. Fonda desperately sought the role, and was supported by Ford and Steinbeck, so Zanuck gave in, provided that Fonda sign a seven-year contract with Fox. Fonda bitterly resented this blackmail, and despised most of the films he had to make. But the role did so much for his career that it seems retrospectively to have been worth the price.

World War II brought Ford into the navy, where he made *The Battle of Midway* (1942), a stirring documentary narrated partly by Fonda, who was himself in the navy a year later. After the war, they immediately reunited for their first Western together, Fox's *My Darling Clementine* (1946), another milestone. It's the story of Wyatt Earp, who becomes marshal of Tombstone in the 1880s, befriends and battles the consumptive, self-destructive Doc Holliday (Victor Mature), begins a romance with an Eastern woman, Clementine (Cathy Downs), and has a showdown with the notorious Clantons at the OK Corral.

Ford turns this familiar tale into a graceful, nostalgic tribute to the adventurous spirit and honorable code of men like Earp, who brought order to the West. Ford's realistic frontier town is a primitive but developing society surrounded by desert; his heroes are posed against clouds and the awesome landscape of Monument Valley, suggesting that they are asserting their courage in a beautiful but foreboding environment.

The signs of civilization are apparent: a traveling Shakespearean actor, ridiculed by the anarchic Clantons and, significantly, delivered to the theater by Earp; the foundations of a church; a dance, held outdoors on the church site on a sunny morning, conveying a sense of vigorous community spirit. In one of Ford's loveliest scenes, Earp and Clementine walk toward the church, as "Shall We Gather at the River" (a Ford favorite) is sung. They join in the dance—with his awkwardness and her grace merging in a symbolic meeting of West and East.

Earp, at once a legendary figure and a real human being, is one of Fonda's magnificent creations. He's the definitive strong, silent cowboy: bashful, slow-moving, but undeniably self-confident. (Fonda's deliberate, cat-like walk has never been so pronounced.) His deadpan and

*MY DARLING CLEMENTINE (1946). With Walter Brennan*

apparent naïveté, like Lincoln's, conceal his sensitivity and shrewdness. He's extremely likable, with his Lincolnesque irony and laconic humor, his transcendent nonchalance, his marvelous habit of trying to keep his balance while leaning backward on two legs of a chair. There's also an obvious sadness and sense of defeat in his expression, suggesting a troubled past.

Above all, he's a noble knight—chivalrous toward Clementine and delivering the land from evil. At first he has the seedy look that often accompanies Fonda's entrances into towns, but, symbolically, he wants a shave, anxious to have a less wild appearance. The barber is interrupted by gunfire and Earp—humorously asking "What kind of a town *is* this anyway?"—must quell the disturbance: law is the prerequisite of even the appearance of civilization.

Still, he's not interested in being marshal until motivated by revenge for his brother's death. But at the

*THE FUGITIVE (1947). In the title role*

same time he has a sense of a greater mission. In a skillfully acted scene reminiscent of *Lincoln,* he looks at his brother's grave and speaks quietly and seriously, vowing to stay around awhile: "Can't tell —maybe when we leave this country, young kids like you will be able to grow up and live safe."

With the defeat of the Clantons (in a gunfight brilliantly staged by Ford), he has succeeded. Setting out to visit his father, he says good-bye to Clementine at the edge of town. Civilization is insured by her decision to stay and start a school; continuity by his vow to return. Like Lincoln, he expresses his love simply ("I sure like that name—Clementine"), then heads into the wilderness. Thus the romance is set against the development of the West: the "double vision of an event" in its immediacy and historical context. Unlike *The Grapes of Wrath*, which has a similar farewell and shot of Fonda on the horizon, this film is optimistic about its hero. Although he's temporarily leaving the community, he'll return to start a family and build the West.

Ford's next film, *The Fugitive* (1947), was based on Graham Greene's *The Power and the Glory*, which was about a "whiskey" priest's living with a woman. But because of screen morality, Ford's character is neither alcoholic nor adulterous. Fonda plays a priest in an unspecified Latin-American police state that has outlawed religion. He hides from the police, vaguely hoping that the church will be reestablished, and is aided by a devout magdalen (Dolores Del Rio). But he's not courageous: when the police search for him among the townspeople, he doesn't admit that he's the priest, even though an innocent hostage will die in his place.

However, his innate integrity asserts itself in typical Fonda fashion. When a dying woman needs him, he gives up a chance to leave the country, and, even when he's found sanctuary in another state, he returns to give the last rites to a wanted criminal (Ward Bond), whose flight has paralleled his own. This leads him into a trap set by a Judas-like informer (J. Carrol Naish). He is executed, but, as is customary with Ford, tradition continues, with the arrival of a new

*THE FUGITIVE (1947). With Dolores Del Rio*

*FORT APACHE (1948). With George O'Brien and John Wayne*

priest to take his place.

Ford is back in the realm of *The Informer*, also written by Dudley Nichols, who tends to be pretentious and preachy. Like the earlier film, it's a heavy-handed Catholic parable (Nichols calls it "an allegory of the Passion Play, in modern terms"), with an almost relentlessly somber mood and pace, and an expressionist style. Gabriel Figueroa's cinematography, with its dazzling compositions, heavy shadows and ethereal lighting, supports Ford's portentous symbolism: typical are close-ups of haloed faces and shadows of men (including Fonda as he enters his church) in crucifixion poses.

The idea was to create a "timeless," universal quality, but the film becomes a series of static (though gorgeous) tableaux. Nevertheless, it does represent the intentions of Ford, who, making his first film as an independent producer-director, was free from studio influence: "It came out the way I wanted to—that's why it's one of my favorite pictures—to me it was perfect . . . the critics got at it, and evidently it had no appeal to the public, but I was proud of my work."*

Fonda, who had played haunted fugitives before, here seems stilted, but his almost constant sadness, solemnity, and bewilderment have

*Quoted in Peter Bogdanovich, *John Ford*, University of California Press, 1968, p. 85

a cumulatively pathetic effect. His concerned look here begins as an expression of worry about his own safety, but eventually it indicates his growing solicitude for others. These combine in his best scene, when he pleads desperately for a bottle of wine (also outlawed), which he needs for mass. He is pitifully humble as he pretends he's an alcoholic desperate for a drink, and progressively more anguished as the official who sells it wants to sit and drink with him, and the bottle is completely drained.

From this Calvary, Fonda went to the U.S. Cavalry in *Fort Apache* (1948). In this, the first in Ford's unofficial "cavalry trilogy" (the other films were *She Wore a Yellow Ribbon* and *Rio Grande*), Fonda plays his most unpleasant character to that time: Colonel Owen Thursday, an arrogant, stubborn martinet who recklessly leads his troops into an Indian massacre. At the time, Fonda said, "Ford is the only man . . . who would have enough imagination to put me into that role. It was a relief to get out of the sort of Alice-in-Wonderland thing they always think of me for."

Thursday, a West Point man, is bitterly disappointed at being "shunted off" to Fort Apache, an isolated frontier outpost. Cold, stiff, and obnoxious, he's immediately contrasted with the spontaneous, warmhearted officers and women at

*With director John Ford in 1971*

the fort (who, naturally, are having a dance when he arrives), and particularly with Captain York (John Wayne), a levelheaded, amiable, experienced cavalryman.

Ford shrewdly combines the traits of a number of previous Fonda characters—sullenness, solemnity, pomposity, naiveté—and brings them to extremes. Fonda adroitly conveys Thursday's stern-faced, iron-jawed manner and monotonously formal, condescending tone. At times his inflexibility is humorous (he maintains his rigid composure even when a chair has collapsed under him), but more often it is destructive. He forbids his daughter (Shirley Temple) to see a lieutenant (John Agar), mostly because he looks down on the young man's lower-class Irish background. And he imposes harsh discipline on the regiment, but doesn't accompany it with compassion or an understanding of the cavalry.

Thursday, contemptuous of the Apaches, ignores York's statements that they are savage only because of the white man's cruelty. (Wayne plays an unusually enlightened man for a 1948 Western.) York arranges a meeting between Cochise and Thursday, but the latter rudely breaks off negotiations, calling the Indian dishonorable. He decides to attack the Apaches, disregarding York's warning that it would be suicidal. His men are hopelessly outnumbered, and York rides in to rescue Thursday. But the colonel wants to rejoin his besieged troops; in the final moments of his life he is ennobled (Ford's theme of "glory in defeat") by this decision, and by apologizing to the men with whom he is about to die.

After systematically destroying the myth of a Custer-like hero, Ford shows York—with whom we are meant to sympathize—addressing reporters and promulgating a legend of Thursday's glorious charge. Ford's message is that the cavalry—and the nation—need to believe in heroes, no matter how stupid they actually were; as in *The Man Who Shot Liberty Valance*, we should "print the legend." Despite the disturbing implications of this cover-up philosophy, Ford supports it with one of his most unforgettable images. As York speaks, he looks out of a window, and superimposed over his face is the reflection of cavalrymen riding: the individual is only a small part of history, of an enduring tradition.

Ford's nostalgia for the camaraderie and romantic heroism of the cavalry is expressed throughout: in the Grand March and dance; the nighttime serenade; the robust Irish humor; the processions and chases across the imposing Monument Valley landscape; and the exciting last stand of a man who is foolish, but is at least committed to his own sense of honor.

The Wayne character took over in the rest of the trilogy, but by then Fonda had left Hollywood for the stage; *Fort Apache* marked a temporary ending to his film career. He did make one more film with Ford, *Mister Roberts*. But that is part of a different chapter in his life.

# SNAKES, SIMPLETONS, AND SOCIAL SIGNIFICANCE

Fonda's films for John Ford between 1939 and 1948 were crucial to the actor's development. But during the forties, he made many additional movies, some of which were routine, while others contributed important facets to his image.

The forties began most promisingly for Fonda, with the January, 1940 release of *The Grapes of Wrath* (as well as the birth of his son Peter in February). But his next film, *Lillian Russell* (1940), indicates why he hated his Fox contract. In this lavish musical biography of the Gay Nineties star, he merely supported Alice Faye in a dull role as her second husband, and was again billed under Don Ameche. It was Zanuck's way of humbling his stars.

Fonda's next Fox assignment, *The Return of Frank James* (1940), was much more fortunate, although Fonda didn't think so at the time because it reteamed him with his least favorite director, Fritz Lang. This was Lang's first color film, and he performed some interesting experiments in combining colors with expressionist light and shadow. As before, Fonda was annoyed by Lang's attention to minute visual details.

The film (which Zanuck reportedly made because fans had demanded a sequel to *Jesse James*) opens with a reprise of Jesse's murder, and follows with a lovely scene in which Frank leads a horse and plow in a gorgeous country setting; again Fonda is a farmer whose peaceful bucolic existence will be destroyed.

When the cowardly Fords are pardoned, Frank sets out to avenge Jesse's death. Accompanied by an admiring teen-ager named Clem (Jackie Cooper), he pursues the murderers from Kansas to Colorado, and even his budding romance with a strong-willed reporter, Eleanor (Gene Tierney), doesn't deter him from his mission. Like the protagonists of Lang's *Fury*, *Rancho Notorious* and *The Big Heat*, he's a man whose hatred becomes an obsessive desire for revenge.

With his cold, blue-eyed gaze, unruffled manner and deliberate way of stalking his prey, Fonda has the look of an implacable avenger. But, as in *Jesse James*, Frank is entirely likable—a gentle, easygoing, tobacco-chewing man of the people and an enemy of the monstrous railroad. Again his actions are always justifiable: he steals only to finance his pursuit, and only from the railroad that caused his family's

*THE RETURN OF FRANK JAMES (1940). As Frank James*

misery. And although a clerk is killed during the holdup, and both Fords die in the course of the film, Frank isn't directly responsible for any death.

In addition, he's another of Fonda's men of conscience. When a loyal servant is unjustly convicted of the clerk's murder, Frank abandons his search and surrenders, knowing that he'll probably be found guilty. His sense of humor is also endearing. When he hears a report of his own death, he remarks, "He had it comin' to him, I reckon." At the trial, he tells the badgering prosecutor, "Sorry—I can't talk without thinkin', not

*THE RETURN OF FRANK JAMES (1940). With Jackie Cooper (left)*

bein' a lawyer." It's an expansion of the subtle, ironic humor he displayed in *Jesse James*, but with the unmistakable addition of Lincoln; Ford's imprint on Fonda was indelible.

Frank's humanity is insured by his concern for Clem, whom he's raised since the boy's outlaw father was killed. This is Fonda's first genuinely parental role, presaging films of almost twenty years later. Frank's tender interludes with Eleanor have the warmth and simplicity of the romances in *Lincoln* and *Clementine*. At the end, when he leaves, she asks if he'll return, and he replies, "There's lots I like about Denver." This has the same quality of unstated emotion as Lincoln's remark to Ann about her hair and Earp's to Clementine about her name: it's the strong, silent Westerner's way of expressing love.

Fonda was back in the Mohawk Valley in Fox's *Chad Hanna* (1940), which, like *The Farmer Takes a Wife* and *Drums Along the Mohawk*, was based on a Walter Edmonds story. An awkward and ingenuous, but resourceful country boy, he joins a circus touring the Erie Canal region in the 1840s, and becomes involved with two equestriennes (Dorothy Lamour and Linda Darnell). Director Henry King's color photography effectively captures the spectacle of the circus and the atmosphere of rural America, but the film was hardly a milestone for Fonda.

If Fonda was unhappy at Fox because of projects such as this, he had cause to rejoice when he was loaned to Paramount for Preston Sturges' screwball comedy, *The Lady Eve* (1941). Sly, sexy and sparkling, it is the most enduring of his non-Ford films of the forties. Like Sturges' other classics made between 1940 and 1944 (including *The Great McGinty* and *Sullivan's Travels*), this updating of Adam and Eve displays the director-writer's magical gifts for clever dialogue, expert comic timing and subtle blending of cynicism and romanticism. Richard Corliss has called it "the most perfectly realized of all his films."

Fonda is Charles ("Hoppsy") Pike, snake expert and scion of a wealthy ale-making family. Returning home on a liner after a year of snake-hunting in the Amazon jungle, he meets Jean (Barbara Stanwyck) and her father (Charles Coburn), a pair of con artists who plan to cheat him in a card game. The innocent succumbs easily to the temptress' charms, but, to her surprise, she also falls for him. After they express their mutual love, he learns from his bodyguard that she's a thief. She claims she was going to tell him, but he is vindictive, and, to save face, he claims that he knew all along and was leading her on.

Deeply hurt, she plans an elaborate revenge, which involves posing as the elegant "Lady Eve Sidwich" and luring him into mar-

*CHAD HANNA (1940). With Dorothy Lamour*

riage. (He doesn't realize she's the same woman, even though she doesn't disguise herself.) On the honeymoon, "Eve" tells lurid stories about previous marriages until, in a state of shock, he leaves her. But she doesn't go through with the rest of her scheme —obtaining a large settlement —because she still loves him. All ends well when Hoppsy, still married, takes another ocean voyage, where he meets Jean again. Grateful because anyone would be better than "Eve," he enters her stateroom. Sturges discreetly leaves them, but the implication is clear: Hoppsy, still deluded, is about to commit what *he* thinks is adultery, but what we—and the censors—know is not.

Sturges took some basic Fonda ingredients—the stern, dour expression; the plaintive whine; the archetypal innocence; the shyness and the dryness—and created a deft, deadpan comic. Fonda is hilarious in the card game, where they hustle him into thinking he's an expert card player; in his dumbfounded reactions upon first seeing "Eve"; in his proposal to her, which he delivers with utmost seriousness, while a horse nudges them; on the honeymoon, where he pompously forgives her and forces a smile, then becomes enraged when she reveals more of her past. Fonda also shows a flair for slapstick and an artful clumsiness,

*THE LADY EVE (1941). With Barbara Stanwyck*

*THE LADY EVE (1941). With Barbara Stanwyck*

as he falls over a sofa, slips into a mud puddle, bumps into things, has various objects fall on him, and is tripped twice by Stanwyck.

Fonda and Stanwyck perform with a spontaneity missing from their other two films together. Two scenes, marking important stages in the initial relationship, are especially noteworthy. Soon after they've met, he kneels to help her put on shoes, and becomes dizzy from the combined effects of her perfume, her legs, and the fact that he's been away from women for so long. After being deliberately seductive, she rebuffs his slight attempt to kiss her, saying that he should be kept in a cage.

Later, after she's been scared by his snake, they return to her cabin so he can comfort her. They sit on the floor and—mostly in one take—perform an amazingly erotic scene. She puts her arms around him and her cheek against his,

*WILD GEESE CALLING (1941). With Joan Bennett*

plays with his hair, and—both to tease him and to hide her growing affection—asks inane questions about snakes and the Amazon. He is stiff, awkward, increasingly frustrated—his eyes staring numbly, his voice breaking into a strangled whimper. After a while, she suddenly says that he can leave; she can sleep peacefully now. "I wish I could say the same," he gulps.

Critics were ecstatic about the film and Fonda was hailed for his suddenly revealed comic talent. But he was less lucky with his next movie, Fox's *Wild Geese Calling* (1941), a rugged outdoors adventure set in the Pacific Northwest in 1895. A sturdy lumberjack, he marries a tough but gold-hearted dance-hall girl (Joan Bennett), and becomes involved in melodramatic action in the Alaskan gold fields.

Fonda complained that after proving he could do "modern stuff," he deserved better from Zanuck than the old "hillbilly roles." Of course, in *Eve*, he had still been the naïve boy next door (his wealth notwithstanding), rather than a worldly sophisticate. In any case, he had nothing to worry about: Hollywood was anxious to accommodate him, especially if it meant repeating successful formulas. He got his wish for "modern stuff" with his next six films, two of which were obvious attempts to recapture *Eve*'s magic.

The easiest way to imitate a hit is to bring together its stars, so he was back with Stanwyck in Columbia's *You Belong to Me* (1941), a slapstick farce about a millionaire playboy who marries a successful doctor. House calls keep interrupting their home life —starting with the wedding night—and Fonda, bored with staying in his palatial mansion all day, becomes irrationally jealous of his wife's male patients. The real evil is in being idle and rich (a carry-over from thirties comedies like *Spendthrift*), and it's not until he finds a way to spend his fortune, like Mr. Deeds, that his other problems are solved.

Warners' *The Male Animal* (1942), directed by Elliott Nugent and based on a play by Nugent and James Thurber, combines Fonda's two major images of the period: the pathetically comic, stepped-upon character and the man forced by circumstances to become a champion of human rights. He's a mild, bespectacled Midwestern college professor facing two crises: his wife (Olivia de Havilland) is too atten-

*YOU BELONG TO ME (1941). With Barbara Stanwyck and Melville Cooper*

*THE MALE ANIMAL (1942). With Jack Carson and Olivia de Havilland*

tive to a visiting former football hero (Jack Carson), and the campus is outraged over his intention to read to his class a letter by the anarchist Vanzetti (as an example of writing, not political philosophy). He proves that an English teacher can be a real hero, when he defies the reactionaries and reads the letter.

Fonda sparkles in his bemused sarcasm toward football, his uncontrollable jealousy, and his long drunk scene in which he extols behaving toward women and rivals like a "male animal," then ineffectually attempts to fight Carson. But while the film is a good satire of athlete worship and machismo, it can't support its serious pretensions about academic freedom, especially since Fonda's climactic plea seems largely motivated by his desire to prove something to his wife.

Still, in the dark days of early 1942, when America had just entered the war, the calm, sincere delivery by the New Deal liberal must have made these lines effective: "I'm fighting for a teacher's right and a student's right, and the rights of everybody in this land. You can't suppress ideas . . . not in this country. Not yet . . . . You know where that leads and where it *has* led in other places. We hold the fortress of free thought and free speech in this place this afternoon . . ."

*RINGS ON HER FINGERS (1942). With Gene Tierney*

*THE MAGNIFICENT DOPE (1942). With Edward Everett Horton and Don Ameche*

Meanwhile, at Fox, Zanuck was living up to his reputation for imitating the success of others. Reportedly jealous of Fonda's luck with Sturges, he screened their film for his writers and said, "Write me a *Lady Eve*." They did, and called it *Rings on Her Fingers* (1942). This time Gene Tierney is the attractive swindler who falls for the bewildered sucker. A gum-cracking salesgirl seeking wealth and excitement, she joins a pair of con artists and poses as their aristocratic daughter in order to lure gullible men. Naturally their first victim is Fonda, a hard-working, upright, naïve clerk whom they cheat out of his life's savings. When Tierney falls in love, she attempts to return the money without his learning about the swindle, and to escape both the police and her unhappy partners.

If this was a thinly disguised plagiarism of *Eve*, Fox's *The Magnificent Dope* (1942) was another *Mr. Deeds*, with Fonda as the seemingly stupid hick who teaches the city slickers how to enjoy life. Although it subscribes to the noble rustic idea, it does effectively satirize another American myth: the Horatio Alger success story, which apparently even the Depression didn't kill.

The fast-talking head of an unsuccessful success school (Don Ameche, finally supporting Fonda) and his cynical fiancée (Lynn Bari, in a Jean Arthur role) decide to improve business by showing that the country's "biggest failure" can be turned into a success. But the man they find (Fonda) is perfectly happy as a failure; he's worked at being lazy and is proud of it. When he becomes attracted to Bari, he takes the course so that she can be proud of him, but eventually he convinces everyone that his laziness is preferable to the pressures of modern, urban civilization, and—what else?—he takes the woman back to the country.

Fonda, as always, is persuasive as the bewildered, whiny country boy; and he's hilarious when trying the hard sell—talking rapidly, telling awful jokes, being obnoxiously aggressive. There are diverting scenes in which he practices his charm-school smiles and speeches, and soothes the city folks with a combination of his special head exercise and his gentle descriptions of easy country living. Walter Lang directed this minor but likable film.

Next was Fox's *Tales of Manhattan* (1942), an ambitious omnibus film directed by Julien Duvivier and scripted by ten writers. A large cast enacts five separate stories, tied together by a dress suit with tails that is passed from one person to another. Fonda appears with Ginger Rogers and Cesar Romero in a farcical episode about a woman caught between two lovers.

Fonda plays his biggest fool in RKO's *The Big Street* (1942), a

*TALES OF MANHATTAN (1942). With Ginger Rogers*

Damon Runyon tale peopled with the author's colorful Broadway guys and dolls. In what may be, except for *King Kong*, the screen's strangest fable of unrequited love, a sincere but hopelessly naïve busboy named Little Pinks (Fonda) has a futile infatuation for a selfish, obnoxious nightclub singer (Lucille Ball), whom he addresses as "Your Highness." Although she treats him like a doormat, he attends to her wishes, sees that she's cared for when her gangster lover permanently cripples her in a fight, and even wheels her from New York to Florida, where she expects to land a millionaire.

This is even more self-sacrifice than Bette Davis went through in *That Certain Woman*, and although Fonda is appealing (if excessively dour) in the early scenes—in which Pinks idolizes his bitchy goddess, tries to build her hopes, and makes excuses for her ill temper—the character's continual self-abasement and utter blindness to her mean nature become too unbelievable for anyone to have portrayed convincingly.

Somehow, in the final scene, the film transcends its implausibilities. To keep her spirit alive, Pinks arranges (through larceny, blackmail, and his friends' strong-arm tactics) a ball in her honor. At last she realizes his devotion, and as he leads her around the dance floor—the crippled woman holding onto him for support and dying in his arms—it suddenly becomes a touching love story.

Fonda now seemed typed as a timid simpleton; one critic remarked, "Certainly there is no other actor who can so perfectly portray dogged, unquestioning devotion." A welcome change came with Fox's *The Ox-Bow Incident* (1943), the message Western that Fonda loves. Actually Darryl Zanuck had been unenthusiastic, believing (correctly) that a story about a lynching would be uncommercial, but director William Wellman liked the novel and persuaded him to do the film.

The critics also predicted box-office failure, but praised the film as timely (there had been recent lynchings in the United States) and honest. Today it seems an odd amalgam of grim, "realistic" subject matter and strangely stylized, non-naturalistic studio settings; of sharply observed characters and grotesque caricatures. And the message is somewhat forced by the victims' innocence: would their hangings be more justifiable if they *were* murderers?

As in *The Grapes of Wrath*, Fonda blends admirably into the ensemble. He's best in the opening, where he creates a vivid portrait of an unpleasant, sardonic

*THE BIG STREET (1942). With Barton MacLane and Lucille Ball*

cowboy. Unshaven, grubby, irritable, Gil Carter drifts into a small Nevada town with his partner (Henry Morgan) and enters a saloon, where he remarks humorously on a risqué painting, quickly becomes drunk, and viciously fights someone because violence makes him feel better.

Carter is a loner who views the group with distrust. When the restless townspeople, led by a demagogue and a few sadists, form a posse to find murdering cattle thieves, he'd rather mind his own business, but he goes along to avoid their suspicion. Initially he questions only their tactics: "I got nothin' particular against hangin' a murderin' rustler. I just don't like doin' it in the dark."

However, he grows in stature, evolving much like Tom Joad. First he becomes the audience's witness—reflecting in his anxious gaze our powerless outrage at hypocritical individuals who seek revenge merely to satisfy their pride and machismo. Then he goes further, arguing with the mob's leader, joining a small group who vote against lynching three men, finally taking direct action as a bully hits Martin (Dana Andrews), one of the accused. The minority's ultimate failure to prevent the hangings symbolizes the impotence of well-meaning people in fighting tyranny unless they can increase in number. In 1943 it was an implied plea for the defense of liberty against fascism.

The final scene, in which Carter reads to the shaken posse a letter written by Martin, recalls *The Grapes of Wrath*. As "Red River Valley" is played mournfully, he says, "Law is the very conscience of humanity . . . what is conscience except a piece of the conscience of all men who ever lived?" Fonda's unhysterical delivery makes even this preaching work; here, as throughout, he embodies the liberal concerns of an era.

His more overt contribution to war propaganda was Fox's *The Immortal Sergeant* (1943), which depicted the British campaign in the Libyan desert, and revived his Milquetoast image. A timid, indecisive journalist who doesn't even have the courage to fight a rival for his girl (Maureen O'Hara), he winds up in the army, where he continually avoids responsibility, even after being promoted to corporal. But when his sergeant (Thomas Mitchell) is killed and he has to take command, he is transformed by events—like other Fonda heroes and like Gary Cooper's Sergeant York—into a courageous fighter.

At the time, Fonda was agonizing over his own role in the war. Because of his age (thirty-seven) and family, he was exempt. Nevertheless, while realizing the possible hardship on his wife and three children, he enlisted in the navy. The decision-making was right out of a Fonda film: "I put it off for a year and then I just

*THE OX-BOW INCIDENT (1943). With Dana Andrews*

*THE IMMORTAL SERGEANT (1943). With Thomas Mitchell*

couldn't face myself. I didn't want to be a hero, but I just couldn't stay out when everyone else was in."

In August 1942, immediately after finishing *Sergeant*, he began his service as an apprentice seaman. But he received a commission, and, after completing a rigorous training near the top of his class, he went to the Pacific in April 1944, as an assistant operations and air combat intelligence officer. Although he never actually saw combat, he served with distinction: upon his discharge in October 1945, he received a Bronze Star, a Presidential Citation and the rank of Lieutenant Senior Grade.

He was reluctant to return to films, but he still had his Fox commitment (three years of which had been used up during his service). Fonda's anti-Fox attitude notwithstanding, it was there he made his first postwar film, *My Darling Clementine*, the strength of which reinsured his box-office viability.

He was less fortunate at RKO with *The Long Night* (1947), Anatole Litvak's inferior remake of Marcel Carné's 1940 film *Le Jour Se Leve (Daybreak)*. One of the forties' numerous moody melodramas, it presents the dark, violent side of

*THE LONG NIGHT (1947).* With Ann Dvorak

*DAISY KENYON (1947). With Joan Crawford*

Fonda's ordinary young man. He's a mill worker, trapped in a dingy tenement room while an army of police and curious crowds mass outside. As he holds off the lawmen, he recalls what led him into this predicament: his romance with a sweet woman (Barbara Bel Geddes), her seduction by an unscrupulous magician (Vincent Price), and Fonda's inability to endure Price's sadistic sneers, leading to a confrontation in which Fonda kills him.

Fonda finally ended his Fox commitment with *Daisy Kenyon* (1947), a triangle drama kept from slipping on its soap by Otto Preminger's intelligent, graceful direction. It's actually a vehicle for Joan Crawford, playing a fashion illustrator who must decide between a wealthy married lawyer (Dana Andrews) and a homespun war veteran (Fonda). She finally chooses Fonda and the more conventional life he seems to represent.

Despite the supporting nature of

the role (perhaps a perverse departing present from Zanuck), Fonda's character is fairly interesting. He's not the simple nice guy that his amiable, polite exterior indicates. Haunted by his wife's accidental death and adjusting uncertainly to civilian life, he's one of the many disturbed veterans found in postwar American films. However, since everyone else in the film is also neurotic, Fonda turns out to be relatively self-possessed, and wins Crawford through some expert amateur psychology: adopting a deceptively passive attitude, which at times is infuriating, but which becomes, in his words, a good "combat tactic."

With several somber films behind him, Fonda probably welcomed the 1948 omnibus comedy *A Miracle Can Happen* (also called *On Our Merry Way*), which teamed him for the first time with James Stewart, and enabled the old friends to relive the genial clowning of their early lean years together. They play down-and-out jazzmen, trying to earn money

*A MIRACLE CAN HAPPEN (ON OUR MERRY WAY) (1948)*. With James Stewart and Dorothy Ford

by fixing an amateur music contest in California, and their slapstick performances stand out delightfully in an otherwise dull film. Their segment, written by John O'Hara, was directed by John Huston and George Stevens, neither of whom desired—or received—screen credit. Fonda liked both directors, but, oddly, never worked with them in any other film.

His next film, *Fort Apache* (1948), was his fortieth. He had come to Hollywood expecting to do a minimum number of films, and had ended up making an average of four a year. As he once remarked, he had easily become "seduced" into contractual obligations; besides, he hadn't found tempting stage roles. In any case, he had, in his view, been sidetracked from his real career, and by 1947 he was ready to return to Broadway.*

In November, he was in New York, hoping to convince Joshua Logan to direct a film of John O'Hara's *Appointment in Samarra*. But Logan would talk only about a comedy he had just written with Thomas Heggen, which was scheduled to be produced by Leland Hayward and directed by Logan on Broadway. Fonda loved it, and immediately asked his agent to get him out of his film commitments.

He signed a one-year contract, believing that his four films yet to be released would keep moviegoers from forgetting him during his brief vacation from Hollywood. Of course he could not foresee that the play—*Mister Roberts*—would be an enormous hit, that there would be others following it, and that he would be away from films for seven years.

*Actually, he had appeared in one Broadway play, in 1937: *Blow Ye Winds*, a comedy-romance about the skipper of a fishing boat who marries a psychologist. The critics liked Fonda, but not the play, and it ran five weeks.

## STAGE INTERLUDE

The ads proclaimed: "Henry Fonda in Person!" The advance sale and excitement were extraordinary. The opening-night audience, on February 18, 1948, was ecstatic, with some standing on their chairs to cheer Fonda. And the reviewers were extravagant with praise, especially for his restrained performance. *Mister Roberts* was unquestionably a critical and commercial success, and happiest of all was its star, who called the opening "the most exciting night of my life," and said, "Mister Roberts was my all-time favorite role. There's nothing that guarantees an actor will ever get a part like that."

Roberts is the popular first officer on the *Reluctant*, a cargo ship a thousand miles from the battle areas in the Pacific—sailing, in his words, "from Tedium to Apathy and back again, with an occasional side trip to Monotony." The war is ending, and he wants to get into combat before it's too late. But his tyrannical captain keeps refusing him a transfer, and it's finally the crew—out of appreciation for his constant efforts on its behalf—which helps him get off the ship. Later, the crew receives a letter stating that he has been killed in the fighting.

Joshua Logan has said that although neither he nor Thomas Heggen had mentioned it to each other, both had thought of Fonda when writing the play; not surprisingly, therefore, Roberts possesses some familiar Fonda traits. He's gentle, compassionate and sincere, and displays the quiet heroism of characters like Earp and Lincoln. Both in his desire to get into the war and in his continual defiance of the captain, he's again the decent man opposing any kind of tyranny.

The play settled in for a long run. By early 1949, Fonda was canceling film roles; he expected to return to Hollywood eventually, but decided to stay with *Roberts* (which he believed was improving with each performance) until it closed.

Plans to make a film version during the summer of 1949, using the original cast, fell through. But Fonda did find time to do a cameo role as a waiter in *Jigsaw* (1949), at the request of the film's star, his friend Franchot Tone.

Fonda's happiness with the play's success was, unfortunately, marred by the disintegration of his marriage. Divorce proceedings were announced at the end of 1949. The following February, Frances Fonda suffered a nervous breakdown and was institutionalized, and on April 14, 1950, she committed suicide.

*On stage in MISTER ROBERTS (1948) with William Harrigan*

*THE CAINE MUTINY COURT MARTIAL (1954). With Robert Gist, Charles Nolte, and John Hodiak*

Fonda finally left the Broadway cast on October 28, 1950, because of a knee operation. In thirty-two months, he had done the play 1,077 times, and had never missed a performance. He next went on national tour, giving another 300 performances, and the *Reluctant* made its last voyage in Los Angeles on August 4, 1951, ending Fonda's amazing three-and-a-half-year association with the play.

Before the tour, on December 28, 1950, he married Susan Blanchard, the twenty-one-year-old stepdaughter of Oscar Hammerstein II. (The marriage lasted until May 2, 1956; there was one daughter, Amy, whom they adopted at birth in November 1953.)

After *Roberts*, Fonda defied expectations that he'd return to films, and immediately found another Broadway play, *Point of No Return*, adapted by Paul Osborn from J.P. Marquand's best-selling novel. Fonda played a bank executive involved in a subtle but vicious competition with a colleague for a higher position. He has spent his life pursuing success, but now that he has to compromise his integrity, self-doubts emerge (a familiar situation in some of Fonda's later films). The play opened on December 13, 1951, and critics again praised his seemingly effortless acting. It ran for 356 performances, closing on November 22, 1952, and then Fonda went on national tour from November 24 to the following May.

Now that he was successful in the theater, Fonda wasn't hurrying back to his movie career. He was scheduled to appear in a musical play of Steinbeck's *Cannery Row*, but instead was cast in Herman Wouk's *The Caine Mutiny Court-Martial*, which opened on January 20, 1954, and gave Fonda the best reviews of his stage career to date. He played Lieutenant Greenwald, assigned to defend Lieutenant Maryk, who led a mutiny against the neurotic Captain Queeg. Through subtle maneuvers, he turns the trial into a character assassination of Queeg, and wins for his client. But, at a celebration, he repudiates his own methods, which he realizes were not justified by the ends.

In all three plays, Fonda was a man of integrity who found it necessary to compromise himself, but whose basic decency emerged.

At least Roberts' compromise was altruistically motivated, but the others acted for expediency and advancement, which in the Fonda moral scheme is a cardinal sin.

When *Caine Mutiny* opened, a film of Wouk's book had already been cast, with Jose Ferrer as Greenwald. But Fonda was more interested in the upcoming film of *Mister Roberts*. It had always been assumed that he would get the role, not only because his stage success had given him a new status in Hollywood, but because to the public, Fonda and Roberts were synonymous.

But Leland Hayward, the film's producer and the man who had first brought Fonda to Hollywood, believed that he had been away from the screen too long, and was no longer a box-office name. He offered the part to William Holden, who refused, saying Fonda should have it, and to Marlon Brando, who is said to have accepted it.

That Fonda finally did get the role was due to his old friend, John Ford, who refused to direct the film without him. On May 29, 1954, Fonda quit his play. After an absence of seven years, he was returning to Hollywood.

If it had not been for *Mister Roberts* (1955), Fonda might never have become a film star again. And once more he was indebted to John Ford, who had made him an important actor in the first place. Unfortunately, however, their reunion was far from joyous. Fonda reportedly had set ideas about the play he had done for so many years, and rebelled against some of Ford's changes, particularly the increased emphasis on slapstick. They argued constantly, and ultimately had a fistfight. Shortly thereafter, Ford left the film anyway, because of illness, and was replaced by Mervyn LeRoy. The dispute was a sad ending to a fruitful relationship, although Fonda did think enough of Ford to appear in Peter Bogdanovich's eloquent documentary tribute, *Directed by John Ford* (1971).

Ford took credit for most of *Roberts*, and though it's hardly one of his major works, much of it displays his distinctive style and vision: the combination of boisterous comedy and sentiment; the vigorous camaraderie among servicemen; the nostalgia for a time just passing; the feeling of the "family" breaking up when Roberts departs; Pulver's upholding tradition by continuing Roberts' defiance of the captain's tyranny. The opening shots, in which Roberts gazes longingly at the task force on the horizon, stunningly express Ford's idea of the individual set against the background of history.

# LAW, POLITICS, AND FATHER FIGURES

When Fonda had left Hollywood, he'd been forty-three. Now he was fifty, and there was a difference —not so much in his appearance, because he still looked in his forties—but in his more mature character. In the stage version of *Roberts*, he had been only eleven years older than David Wayne, who played Pulver. Now he was twenty years older than the film's counterpart (Jack Lemmon), and the image was closer to that of a parent. Therefore Roberts, while young enough to be a rebel and a genuine friend to the younger crewmen, is also mature enough to convey the air of adult authority and to be the crew's mediator and father figure. The friend-father combination recurs in several subsequent films.

In *Roberts*, Fonda has another self-effacing role, because he is upstaged not only by the crew's tumultuous activities, but by two other principal actors: Jack Lemmon (who won an Oscar)—lecherous, loquacious, always on the verge of exploding; and James Cagney as the captain—sputtering in rage and loudly proclaiming his hatred for "smaht college boys" like Roberts.

*MISTER ROBERTS (1955). In the title role*

*MISTER ROBERTS (1955). With James Cagney*

Fonda stands through all this with extreme poise, like the center of a raging hurricane, and neatly balances gentleness and strength, compassion and contempt, subtle sarcasm and open defiance. There are poignant scenes: his agonized confidence to the ship's doctor (William Powell) about his longing to get into combat; his farewell to the men, which is properly restrained in its pathos. His most humorous moment occurs when, unbearably depressed at the war's passing him by, he suddenly rebels: his eyes bulging out and his face glowing with inspiration, he marches up to the captain's beloved palm tree and tosses it overboard.

The critics applauded him, and said that he now seemed to *be* Roberts. The film was a huge commercial success, and Fonda was a star once more, in as great a demand as ever. It was as though he had never been away.

His absence had occurred during Hollywood's most traumatic period, caused by the challenge of television and the antitrust actions divorcing theaters from studios. The industry was becoming decentralized, with growing numbers of small, independent films (many of them shot in New York) and huge international co-productions. Fonda easily adapted to both of these, since he had never relished the tightly organized studio system anyway. In addition, he was no longer exclusively a film actor; for the rest of his career, Fonda would move freely between movies and plays.

And he accommodated himself as well to television. He had wanted to play circus clown Emmett Kelly since the thirties, and had bought the rights to his autobiography. On March 27, 1955, he appeared in a half-hour television film, *The Clown*, which traced the early years in Kelly's career. The clown himself supervised the routines and makeup, and *Life* magazine, observing that Fonda was Kelly's exact likeness, said that he "lowers his eyes with the same hangdog look and ambles around with the same air of epic lassitude." On May 30, 1955, Fonda appeared in a live television production of *The Petrified Forest*, playing, of course, the sensitive idealist who clashes with a vicious gangster. (Humphrey Bogart recreated his stage and screen role.)

Fonda returned to the stage and to Omaha in 1955 to do a benefit performance of Clifford Odets' *The Country Girl*, for the Community Playhouse. It co-starred another Playhouse graduate, Dorothy McGuire, and featured his daughter Jane in her professional debut. Jane also appeared in *The Male Animal* when her father returned to Cape Cod in August 1956 to do the play in Falmouth and Dennis.

The actor's ability to make

WAR AND PEACE (1956). With Audrey Hepburn

*WAR AND PEACE (1956). With Lea Seidel, Barry Jones, May Britt, Audrey Hepburn, and Sean Barrett*

smooth transitions from one medium to another is indicated by the fact that his next film, which opened while he was in the modest Cape Cod stock production, was one of the biggest epics of the fifties: the three-and-a-half-hour, $5,500,000 American-Italian production of *War and Peace* (1956), in which he played Pierre. The film, directed by King Vidor, skims lightly over Tolstoy, eliminating and simplifying characters and ignoring much of the philosophy. But it is a grand spectacle, with the Battle of Borodino and Napoleon's retreat from Moscow in the snow standing among the cinema's most stunning sequences.

Vidor has written of many disagreements with Fonda, but the actor's major arguments were with the producer, Dino De Laurentiis, who wanted him to play Pierre as a handsome young man. Since Tolstoy's Pierre is large and homely, Fonda wanted at least to use padding, but this wasn't allowed. He did wear spectacles, which De Laurentiis kept telling him to remove, and which Fonda put back on whenever the producer left the set.

Fonda was right, because he does seem too attractive, and his telling Natasha (Audrey Hepburn) that he would ask for her love if he were handsome makes little sense. His attempts at capturing Pierre's awkwardness are only slightly more successful; by now the bumbler of *The Lady Eve* has become a mature, graceful man, and his clumsiness seems forced.

He does convey the character's gentleness, and his earnest desire to discover "what happiness is, what value there is in suffering, why men go to war." Like other Fonda heroes, he begins as an observer who asks questions, and gradually becomes transformed by events. He blunders into a duel, which he wins accidentally, and he wanders all over the Borodino battlefield, trying to study war first-hand. Embittered by the fighting, he curses Napoleon, but cannot carry out his intention to kill the French leader. Only through his ordeal as a prisoner of war does he finally attain self-knowledge and strength.

His relationship with Natasha is in the friend-father mold of Fonda's fifties movies. Natasha, who seems flighty but possesses an underlying maturity, views him as a confidant, brother and—despite his helplessness—parental figure. Their complex feelings about each other are implied in the film's loveliest scene —a quiet walk and conversation in a meadow—where both suppress expressions of love. They go on to other, tragic relationships, and it's not until after they have survived the war that they can build a life together.

Fonda's role as father figure is quite explicit in *The Tin Star* (1957), a Western in which he finds *two* surrogate sons. At first, though, he's a loner: his wife and child have died, and he now leads the rootless life of a bounty hunter. Weary, unshaven, as seedy as in *The Ox-Bow Incident*, he rides into town bearing an outlaw's body. He has to stay until

*THE TIN STAR (1957). With Anthony Perkins*

*WARLOCK (1959). With Dolores Michaels*

he can collect the reward—a visit which doesn't please the townspeople. But he takes their antagonism stoically: he's used to being an outcast.

Again Fonda progresses from alienation to an understanding of responsibility. He befriends a widow (Betsy Palmer) and her half-Indian son, who are ostracized by the town, and whom he sees as a substitute family. And, despite his better judgment, he's persuaded by the town's greenhorn sheriff (Anthony Perkins) to teach him how to shoot. Fonda also dispenses fatherly advice, urging Perkins to quit. Meanwhile, Perkins keeps trying to get Fonda to wear a badge, but Fonda would rather be on his own. When a lynch mob threatens the jail, Fonda finally takes the badge, but Perkins is able to take care of himself, and Fonda looks on with parental pride. At the end, he leaves with his new family, planning to become a sheriff elsewhere.

The film was directed with an expert sense of composition by Western veteran Anthony Mann. And though Dudley Nichols' script, which borrows from *Shane* and *High Noon*, is didactic, it's also humorous: Fonda, saving Perkins' life, says, "Excuse me for buttin' in, sheriff, but you forgot to sign my claim"; and his running remarks about Perkins' inexperience are amusing. There's also a touching scene in which he recalls what made him a bounty hunter—he needed money in a desperate attempt to save his family—and Fonda, speaking in the third person, does it with finely judged restraint.

In *Warlock* (1959), set in the 1880s, Fonda is another itinerant gunslinger with a killer's reputation. He's still basically on the side of law—the darker side of Fonda's Westerner doesn't fully emerge until the late sixties—but his character is more complex than in *The Tin Star*. The town of Warlock, besieged regularly by a gang, hires him as an extra-legal marshal (a kind of super-vigilante). He is accompanied by a gambler (Anthony Quinn) who worships him because of his fast draw. Here Fonda is less a father figure than the object of a homosexual attraction, which is implied but not explored.

He routs the gang, one of whose members (Richard Widmark) stays behind and becomes the legal deputy sheriff; he represents real law, while Fonda stands for the rule of the old heroic, individualistic gunman. Throughout, Fonda, although assured and authoritative, is also overwhelmingly melancholy: he realizes that his days are fading. In their showdown, he outdraws Widmark twice, but doesn't shoot. Bowing to the inevitability of established law, he throws down his guns and leaves town. Unlike *The Tin Star*, the film ends with Fonda as rootless as at the beginning. He has to keep going, because even though times are changing, there will be enough towns needing his kind of law to last his lifetime.

Fonda's most subtle performances of the fifties are in two other films dealing with justice and the law. The first, Alfred Hitchcock's *The Wrong Man* (1956), resurrected the innocent victim of *You Only Live Once* and *Let Us Live*. Like the latter, it was based on a true incident: in 1952, Manny Balestrero, a hard-working, honest musician, was mistakenly identified as a hold-up man, then arrested, imprisoned and tried. There was a mistrial, and before the second trial began the real criminal was caught. In the meantime, however, the horrible ordeal of trying to prove his innocence—during which two potentially helpful witnesses died—had caused his wife to suffer a breakdown.

As François Truffaut points out, the story was a real-life illustration of a favorite Hitchcockian theme: an

*THE WRONG MAN (1956). Manny Balestrero is arrested.*

innocent man accused on the basis of circumstantial evidence and systematically stripped of his defenses. And although the film doesn't have the richness of the four Hitchcock masterpieces that followed it in succession, it does express some of their concerns: madness (*Vertigo*, *Psycho*), the confusion of identity and loss of individuality (*North by Northwest*), and, most important, the feeling of helplessness in a precarious universe (*The Birds*).

Through his matter-of-fact depiction of irrational events, Hitchcock creates a Kafkaesque nightmare. At times he approaches documentary in his painstaking observation of Balestrero's humiliation: the arrest, fingerprinting, lineup, questioning by unctuously polite detectives, incarceration. All of this is enhanced by a rigorous style and the use of actual locations. But Hitchcock also abandons objectivity with frequent shots from his victim's perspective, intensifying the feeling that it could happen to *us*.

Fonda was perfectly cast, because the honesty automatically associated with his persona makes us sympathetic from the start. He is the quintessential American family man: pleasant (though not especially intelligent), devoted to his wife, understanding but properly firm with his children, ordinary and colorless. The normalcy of his marriage provides the basis for the horror of its disintegration. The wife (beautifully played by Vera Miles) descends from bitterness to depression to catatonia, as he looks on in confusion. At the end he tries desperately to communicate with her, but it is useless, and our direct confrontation with insanity is as frightening as it is with James Stewart in *Vertigo* and Anthony Perkins in *Psycho*.

Unlike Lang in *You Only Live Once*, Hitchcock has his victim surrender to fate, and he is ultimately rescued only by the power of prayer. When Balestrero is most despondent he prays, and Hitchcock dissolves slowly from his face to the criminal, who is about to be captured. The implication is that belief in God saved him—a somewhat passive solution. Fonda effectively realizes Hitchcock's conception; although he is occasionally angry, through most of the film he looks dazed, bewildered, frightened, melancholy. The chilling scene in which he finally confronts his double and bitterly says, "Do you

*12 ANGRY MEN (1957). As Juror No. 8*

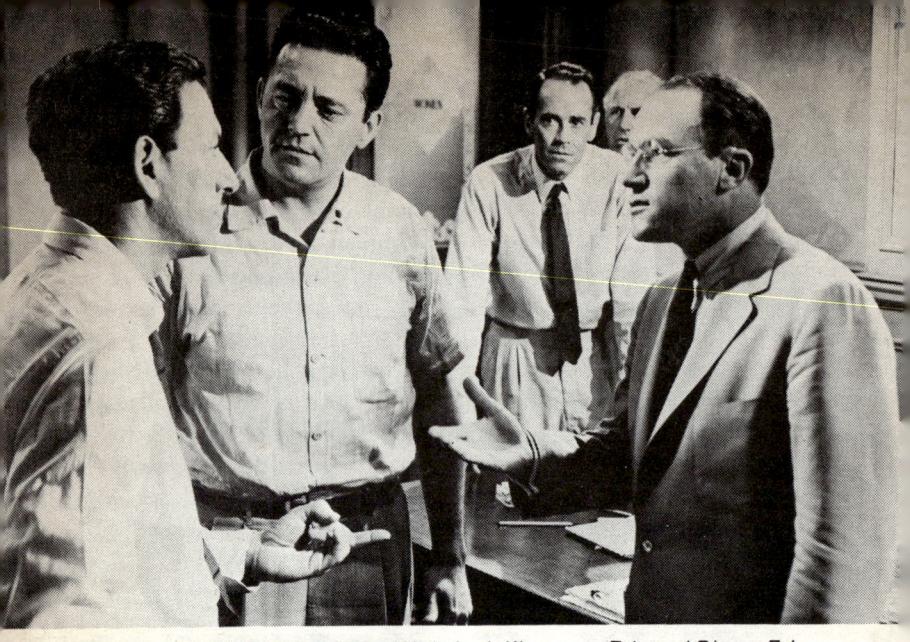

*12 ANGRY MEN (1957). With Jack Klugman, Edward Binns, Ed Begley, and E.G. Marshall*

realize what you've done to my wife?" is a welcome cathartic release from his almost maddening passivity.

The exploration of justice continues in *12 Angry Men* (1957), one of the few films Fonda mentions with pride, and one that is often associated with him. Fonda co-produced it with Reginald Rose, who adapted the script from his 1954 television play. As director they chose Sidney Lumet, another television veteran, who had never made a film. The result was one of the most acclaimed movies of the year.

Fonda has praised Lumet because of his "total communication with an actor. Actors working with Lumet feel that they have given their best performance." He says that *12 Angry Men* was the closest he ever came in movies to the satisfaction of a theatrical performance, because Lumet rehearsed it for two weeks, and staged complete run-throughs. Although the film was shot out of sequence (it is set almost entirely in one room, necessitating intricate planning of camera setups), Fonda believes they could have performed it on stage.

The drama concerns the conflicts among the members of an all-male jury deciding the fate of a teen-ager accused of killing his father. At first all but one of the jurors vote for conviction. The holdout, an architect (Fonda), doesn't necessarily believe the boy is innocent, but feels that there may be a reasonable doubt, and that the accused deserves the dignity of a discussion ("We're talking about somebody's life here . . . . Supposing we're wrong?"). Through his patient, reasonable analysis of the case, he changes everybody's mind.

It's all very unsubtle, with little doubt as to how we should feel or what the outcome will be. At the opening, we see the boy—an emaciated, pitiful, frightened product of the slums—and we are immediately sympathetic. The very presence of Fonda, with his innate probity (as well as a white suit identifying him as the hero), convinces us that the others are wrong. The most uncomfortable contrivance is that his methodical examination of the evidence reveals many obvious flaws that are too obvious to have been overlooked at the trial or by all of the other jurors.

But the contrivances do not detract completely from the drama. The film's confinement to the sweltering jury room creates a palpable tension and claustrophobia, and Lumet's efficient camerawork and editing make an essentially static situation dynamic. As Fonda argues, exposing the prejudices, vindictiveness, insecurities, and hidden strengths of the others, Lumet provides a memorable ensemble: a bully (Lee J. Cobb), unconsciously seeking revenge on his own rebellious son; a bigot (Ed Begley), who thinks all minorities are "trash"; a

*STAGE STRUCK (1958). With Susan Strasberg*

*THE MAN WHO UNDERSTOOD WOMEN (1959). With Leslie Caron*

cold-blooded stockbroker (E.G. Marshall); and various other narrow-minded, selfish or simply apathetic New York types.

The most obvious parallel is *The Ox-Bow Incident*, with Fonda as the individualist who refuses to go along with the lynch mob's verdict. But now the character is mature, thoughtful, an island of calm in a sea of "angry men." Fonda is persuasive as he calmly raises doubts ("I'm just saying it's *possible*"), performs logical demonstrations, becomes more excited and confident when he is himself convinced of the boy's innocence. If Balestrero was the model of Fonda's decent but inarticulate victim, juror number eight is the model of his articulate fighter—the concerned liberal, the enemy of bigotry, the voice of conscience.

Purely as a favor to Lumet, Fonda appeared in his second film, *Stage Struck* (1958), a remake of *Morning Glory* in which he is a combination of father figure and lover to Susan Strasberg. He plays the old Adolphe Menjou role of a suave theatrical producer who takes advantage of a hopeful young actress. She idolizes him and thinks that their one-night affair is something more, but he rejects her. In the end, though, romance is only secondary: she substitutes for the star on opening night, becomes a success, and realizes that her only love is the Theater. And Fonda is there to bestow fatherly congratulations.

The film is one long cliché, and Strasberg is terrible in Katharine Hepburn's Oscar-winning role; the scene in which she awes a roomful of experienced theater people with a supposedly inspired recitation of Juliet's balcony speech is ludicrous. Fonda is unconvincing as a smooth playboy, but most of the time he makes his character a basically sincere, thoughtful man and a paternal comforter, which he does well. And if his dressing room pep talk ("You're a hungry little girl—the theater's offering you a feast") misses Warner Baxter's urgency in *42nd Street*, it is reasonably authoritative.

The theater offered Fonda something less than a feast with *Two for the Seesaw*, his first Broadway play since 1954. This two-character comedy, which opened on January 16, 1958, occasioned a legendary dispute between Fonda and playwright William Gibson (which Gibson later recorded in *The Seesaw Log*). From the start, Fonda considered his character—a lonely Omaha lawyer who has an unlikely affair in New York with an emancipated young Bronx woman—too self-pitying, too self-indulgent, and too dull compared with the woman.

Gibson promised to make changes, but despite many rewrites, which meant the agony of last-minute memorizing, Fonda was never comfortable with the role: "Jerry never came off, and it was the *hardest* work I ever did." Considering the bitterness of their fight, it is surprising that the play was a big hit, and that the critics liked Fonda. However, most of them concentrated on Anne Bancroft, the explosive co-star making her Broadway debut. That she received so much attention perhaps bears out Fonda's reservations.

In *Stage Struck* he helped make Strasberg a star, and he does the same for Leslie Caron in *The Man Who Understood Women* (1959), where the Pygmalion-Galatea relationship is much more obvious. He is a fading Hollywood "boy wonder" who turns a nice young woman into a movie queen, thus putting himself once more at the top of the industry. They get married, but he is so preoccupied with making her a great actress that the marriage is never even consummated. This drives her into an affair, which makes Fonda so insanely jealous that he almost murders her.

Adapted from Romain Gary's novel *The Colors of the Day* by director Nunnally Johnson, the film is an uncertain blend of satire, farce and melodrama. But Fonda is enjoyable, particularly when he mocks

*ADVISE AND CONSENT (1962). As Robert Leffingwell*

the Hollywood rat race—a sentiment that must have appealed to him. The role also gave him a strange variety of costumes; as he pictures himself to be a great screen lover, he becomes a famous bullfighter, a sheik, and a Pagliacci clown (with white clown makeup).

After this film, Fonda was away from the screen for almost three years. But this wasn't as noticeable as his previous absence, because it had been clearly established that Fonda would not restrict himself to films. In addition, he did appear regularly on a half-hour NBC television series, *The Deputy*, which premiered on September 12, 1959, and ran for two seasons, totaling seventy-eight episodes. Produced and half-owned by Fonda, the series was an outgrowth of *The Tin Star*, with Fonda as a marshal who helps a young deputy (Allen Case). Actually Fonda was seen throughout in only a handful of episodes, although he did brief scenes in all of them. Some critics and viewers felt cheated, but Fonda reasoned that since the marshal covers a wide territory, one should not expect him always to be in one town, and besides, "the marshal is always 'there,' even if you don't actually see him. His presence is just felt." This couldn't hide the fact that the series capitalized on Fonda's name without his really starring in it. In any event, when NBC wanted to make it an hour-long show, with Fonda appearing more extensively, he refused, thinking that it would tie him down to the exclusion of everything else. The show went off the air in 1961.

He also continued in the theater. In December 1959 he opened in Robert Anderson's *Silent Night, Lonely Night*, as a lonely, sensitive man with a mentally ill wife. He meets a woman (Barbara Bel Geddes) with a troubled marriage at an inn on Christmas Eve, and they share one night's love and companionship. The play received lukewarm reviews (with which Fonda agreed), although his performance was commended. It closed in March 1960.

In December 1960 he opened in Ira Levin's comedy *Critic's Choice*, playing a drama critic faced with the problem of reviewing his wife's play, which he thinks is terrible. The play was based indirectly on drama critic Walter Kerr and his wife Jean, and Kerr himself reviewed it. He didn't like Levin's work, but complimented Fonda, saying that he looked and acted like a critic, and that "he is so full of integrity he should be Secretary of State."

Fonda as Secretary of State? The idea seemed logical; after all, he had already played a president (albeit as a young man), and now he seemed such an image of mature, fatherly

*ADVISE AND CONSENT (1962). With Eddie Hodges*

authority that one would naturally think of him in a post of national leadership.

At least Otto Preminger thought so, and cast Fonda as Robert Leffingwell, the nominee for Secretary of State, in *Advise and Consent* (1962), an ambitious, visually exciting adaptation of Allen Drury's enormously popular Pulitzer Prize novel (which had also been adapted as a play in 1960). Fonda has top billing, and is the focus of the plot. But, typically, he submerges his personality into a large cast of vivid characters and into a complex series of events; although his presence does dominate, he has a relatively brief role.

Drury's novel, with its thinly disguised allusions to actual politicians, had a patently conservative, anti-intellectual bias: Leffingwell was an arrogant, prevaricating left-wing egghead (Alger Hiss?) who deserved to be rejected. Preminger is a liberal, but ends up largely neutralizing the issues. Leffingwell does lie about having attended Communist meetings, but only to protect a former associate, and even this falsehood bothers him enough to ask the President to withdraw his name. At the same time there's an implication of his ambitiousness and moral flabbiness, because he isn't quite noble enough to withdraw on his own.

On balance, though, he does emerge as more a hero than a villain; as *Time* observed, "No proof is offered that Leffingwell is fit or unfit to be Secretary of State, but the grieving spaniel eyes of Henry Fonda transmit their customary message: simpleness is next to godliness." During his testimony before the subcommittee, he conveys an unmistakable forthrightness and dignity. Speaking soberly, with measured tones, he's the essence of composure amid all of the intrigue and high-pitched emotions.

Fonda is best in a clash with Charles Laughton, playing a zealously right-wing Southern senator, whom he calls a nineteenth-century rabble rouser. Arguing for diplomacy in the Cold War, he says, "I believe it's dangerous to negotiate survival with pride determining our attitude." Interestingly, although both sides view him as representing a specific political principle, Leffingwell does not see himself as a fighter for any cause. Even when he dabbled in Communism, he was confused rather than committed, and, significantly, he never joined the party.

At the end, the Senate is deadlocked, the President is dead, and his successor decides to select his own nominee. Thus Fonda never became Secretary of State. But in *The Best Man* (1964), adapted by Gore Vidal from his play, Fonda is a *former* Secretary of State vying for a presidential nomination. The setting is a frenzied 1964 convention, depicted with an astute sense of atmosphere by director Franklin Schaffner.

When Vidal's witty, cynical satire

*ADVISE AND CONSENT (1962). With Burgess Meredith and Paul Stevens*

*THE BEST MAN (1964). With Margaret Leighton*

had been seen on Broadway in 1960, its characters had suggested real politicians: William Russell, an idealistic liberal whose intellectualism makes him indecisive and a loser, resembled Stevenson; Joe Cantwell, an opportunistic conservative who uses smears and anti-Communist rhetoric, was modeled after Nixon. They had less exact equivalents in 1964, but, ironically, they do relate to the 1972 campaign: Russell suggests McGovern (his past breakdown makes him part-Eagleton) and Cantwell is again Nixon (his theft of Russell's psychiatric records has obvious analogies).

Fonda, as Russell, extends his cultivated egghead characterization from *Advise and Consent*. As in Preminger's film, both sides are corrupt, willing to smear each other. Also, as before, the casting of Fonda automatically makes the liberal more heroic than he was in the original source. Fonda again goes along with tactics he knows are wrong ("This is exactly the sort of thing I went into politics to stop. All the business of gossip instead of issues, personalities instead of policies . . . one by one, these compromises, these small corruptions, destroy character"), but this time he regains his principles and withdraws from the race.

Fonda gives one of his finest performances, suggesting a complex blend of integrity and corruption, exultation and ruefulness. Thoughtful and compassionate, he is also gently sarcastic toward Cantwell and eventually about himself. At times he seems detached from the machinations, looking at everything with amusement, as a defense against his realization that he's beginning to like politics.

In his confrontations with Cantwell (whom Cliff Robertson makes a terrifying embodiment of evil), he expresses surprise at his own tactics, and acts more with regret than in anger. His idealism is most convincing when, releasing his delegates to a dark horse in order to stop Cantwell, he says, "You have no responsibility toward anybody or anything. And that is a tragedy in a man and it is a disaster in a president."

But we can also agree with the Trumanesque, plain-speaking ex-president (Lee Tracy), who observes that Russell is indecisive and undynamic. And we can even sympathize with Cantwell when he tells Russell, "You don't understand

*THE BEST MAN (1964). With Cliff Robertson*

*FAIL SAFE (1964). As the President*

politics . . . the country and the way it is and the way we are. You're a fool." In addition, it's difficult to discern exactly what Russell *does* represent, except a vague progressivism; again Fonda seems to be in a fight without really believing strongly in a specific cause. This is because Vidal sees issues as unimportant to the voters; only personalities and methods matter. His choice is between an unrealistic, unfocused liberal and a pragmatic, vicious conservative, with a compromise candidate who's a nonentity. It adds up to a hopeless, though perversely entertaining, view of politics.

Despite flaws in both Leffingwell and Russell, Fonda emerged as the most trustworthy politician in movies. In fact he was asked to play the President in both *Seven Days in May* and the Broadway musical *Mr. President*. But Fonda had another commitment: the film of Burdick and Wheeler's best-selling novel, *Fail Safe* (1964), in which he played, naturally, the President.

Like Stanley Kubrick's black comedy *Dr. Strangelove* (released earlier in the year), *Fail Safe* envisions a holocaust triggered by failure in our complicated nuclear deterrent system, although here a mechanism, not a psychotic general, is at fault—and here, everything is utterly serious and cinematically rather conventional.

When bombers are accidentally directed toward Moscow, the President communicates directly with the Soviet premier, hoping to avoid catastrophe and to convince him that it *was* an accident. Tension increases as neither side can stop the planes. When the bombs destroy Moscow, the President, to show good faith, obliterates New York City in exchange—a finale made extremely chilling by Lumet's rapid montage.

Fonda plays all of his scenes with only one other character, an interpreter (Larry Hagman), and in only a tiny, bare, cell-like room. The image is one of isolation, which is ironic, since his actions are affecting the entire world. Yet with nothing less than the fate of mankind at stake, it is somehow reassuring that the man upon whom we depend is Henry Fonda. No longer the vacillating idealist of *The Best Man*, he's solidly, resolutely in control.

The actor has never been more intense, as he paces the room; patiently but firmly questions his advisers over the phone; sits deep in thought, suddenly aged by his burden; desperately tries to convince the wing commander, trained to ignore all voice communication, to turn back ("Damn it, this is the President!"); decisively orders that the planes be shot down; converses with the premier, speaking loudly, clearly, steadily—his almost monotonously dry voice appropriate to the occasion, when every choice of word and tone becomes significant.

Fonda— with his surpassing sincerity, his mournful expression—is the ideal President for such a crisis, the quintessential father figure. This perfect leader seems capable of making the most immediate decisions while being constantly aware of the overall view, and his final reasoning with the premier is a suitable culmination of Fonda's concerned pleas over the years: "We're paying for our mutual suspicions . . . but the wall must be broken down . . . we're responsible for what happens to us. Today we had a taste of the future. Do we learn from it, or do we go on the way we have?"

Probably nobody else could have made the hot-line conversations more convincing, and yet one cannot help remembering Kubrick's recognition that any attempt to maintain extreme sanity in the face

*SPENCER'S MOUNTAIN (1963). With Maureen O'Hara*

of such universal madness is grotesquely funny. As Fonda speaks, one almost hears Peter Sellers' similarly dry voice in *Strangelove,* uttering lines like, "Listen, how do you think *I* feel about it, Dimitri?" and, through no fault of Fonda's, at times the scenes become unintentionally humorous. Fonda himself says he "flipped over" *Strangelove,* and that if he had seen Kubrick's film first, he would have been unable to do *Fail Safe.*

Fonda is the ultimate father figure in a more literal sense, in *Spencer's Mountain* (1963), where he heads a family of nine children. Based on a novel by Earl Hamner, the film is something of a prototype for Hamner's television series, *The Waltons,* and another Fonda vehicle about the supposed virtues of the bucolic life. The Spencers are a poor but happy clan, living in the Wyoming mountain country, who sacrifice so that the oldest son, Clayboy (James MacArthur), can be the first to attend college. It's puerile and rather dishonest family entertainment in the Disney tradition, except that the leering emphasis on adolescent discovery of sex shows the unmistakable touch of director-scriptwriter Delmer Daves (*A Summer Place, Parrish*).

Fonda, back in the territory of *The Trail of the Lonesome Pine,* is colorful as the earthy, amiable patriarch who works hard in a quarry, dreams of building a house on the mountain, refuses to attend church, is ambivalent toward civilization, and enjoys loafing and making love to his wife (Maureen O'Hara). His character is summed up in a speech he makes against preachers: "They don't allow drinkin' or smokin', card playin', pool shootin', dancin', cussin', or huggin', kissin' and lovin', and I'm for all of them things."

Reportedly, Fonda did this film at the insistence of his agents, who thought that he should appear more frequently on screen. They may have been influenced by the failure of his previous Broadway play, Garson Kanin's *A Gift of Time*. Although Fonda has called it "one of the most beautiful experiences I have ever had in my life," many thought that the subject—a man dying of cancer who finally commits suicide—was depressing. (Olivia de Havilland, appearing opposite him for the first time since *The Male Animal* in 1942, was his noble and loving wife.) The play opened on February 22, 1962 and lasted ninety-one performances.

*Spencer's Mountain*, on the other hand, was a big hit. But Fonda thought that nothing justified the film, especially when he learned that his agents had chosen it over Edward Albee's play *Who's Afraid of Virginia Woolf?*, without even having informed him that Albee had offered the role. He would have been ideal as the intelligent, henpecked college teacher, and the loss of the role was heartbreaking: "I think I would have given up any role I've ever played—Tom Joad or Mr. Roberts, any of them—to have had a chance at that part." (Later, there was speculation that he would co-star with Bette Davis in the film, but when Elizabeth Taylor was cast, Richard Burton went along.)

*Generation*, his next Broadway play, was no *Virginia Woolf*. It was inevitable that the parental figure would find himself in something dealing with "the generation gap." In this successful comedy by William Goodhart, which opened on October 6, 1965, Fonda played a square who tries to understand his daughter's Greenwich Village life-style. Since the daughter was about Jane Fonda's age (twenty-seven), some said that the conflict reflected his own family difficulties, which was making too much of a trivial play.

On December 2, 1965, during the run of *Generation*, Fonda married his fifth wife, Shirlee Adams. He was sixty; she was thirty-three. At least in his marriage, which is still successful, there seemed to be no generation gap.

## HEROES AND ANTI-HEROES

By the sixties, Fonda had become an institution. One indication of this was the frequency with which he was given cameo roles in super-productions, where a well-established persona was often needed for instant characterizations. Even in brief appearances, Fonda gave the impression of having created fully rounded portrayals.

For example, in *The Longest Day* (1962), Darryl F. Zanuck's massive, $10,000,000 recreation of D-Day, he projects an air of assurance and authority as General Theodore Roosevelt; and in *How the West Was Won* (1963), the Cinerama sagebrush spectacular, he is intriguingly offbeat as a grizzled, long-haired, long-mustached buffalo hunter who helps the film's hero (George Peppard) protect railroad workers from Indians.

Fonda also appears in two brief but vivid scenes of Otto Preminger's epic-length World War II drama, *In Harm's Way* (1965). An admiral who restores John Wayne to his deserved command, he has an ironic, Lincolnesque tone as he says (with a charming Southern accent), "Well—now we all know that the navy is never wrong . . . but in this case they was a little weak on bein' right."

He also stands out in another World War II epic, *Battle of the Bulge* (1965), although, like everyone else in this Cinerama extravaganza, he has a rather small role. The emphasis is on action and roller-coaster thrills, with little attempt at serious character study. Fonda, a lieutenant colonel, fights as if he were battling Indians or outlaws on the frontier: he says that the Germans' major mistake was that "They made me mad at them." The film implies that the Nazis lost the battle almost entirely because of his heroic daring in undertaking air reconnaissance without orders.

With his thoughtful countenance and restrained authority, Fonda makes it all somehow convincing. He excels in his clashes with an arrogant colonel (Dana Andrews), who refuses to believe his warnings of a major Panzer assault. Fonda is once more the determined individualist, impatient with short-sighted authority. With the insistence of his juror in *12 Angry Men*, he maintains that "they *could* be wrong."

While in Europe for *Battle*, Fonda did *The Dirty Game* (1966), a three-segment international production about espionage. In his section, directed by Terence Young (of James Bond fame), Fonda plays, for a change, a non-American. He is an undercover agent named Kourlov,

*THE LONGEST DAY (1962). As Brig. Gen. Theodore Roosevelt*

BATTLE OF THE BULGE (1965). With Robert Ryan and Dana Andrews

who escapes from the Russians with vital secrets for the American intelligence chief (Robert Ryan). He reaches their rendezvous point a day early, and when his hiding place is exposed, he is murdered. Fonda skillfully imparts the world-weariness and anxiety of a spy who came in from the cold.

He returned to World War II with a cameo in Robert Aldrich's Cinerama adventure, *Too Late the Hero* (1970). A navy captain, he assigns a rebellious lieutenant (Cliff Robertson) to a British Army group, which is ordered to capture a Japanese radio site and send false information about Allied movements. Fonda's unemotional expression conceals the fact that the mission is virtually suicidal.

Fonda continued to get leading roles as well, but sometimes he had to settle for less. In *Sex and the Single Girl* (1964), he was relegated to supporting "younger generation" performers Natalie Wood and Tony Curtis. The film, co-written by, of all people, novelist Joseph Heller (*Catch-22*), turns Helen Gurley Brown's "how to" book into a comedy that actually contains some good satire (on scandal magazines and psychologists) before it settles into a tired, tasteless, will-she-or-won't-she sex farce.

Fonda and Lauren Bacall, playing a constantly bickering married couple, contribute some of the best scenes. Fonda is amusing as he storms out of the house, grabs the drink that neighbor Curtis holds out as a matter of routine, complains "I hate the woman I love," and swears that he never looks at other women, even though his job as stocking manufacturer gives him an excuse to stare constantly at women's legs. A complicated series of screwball events leads him to be arrested unjustly—a traditional Fonda situation now played for laughs.

Since the sixties, aging stars like Stewart, Wayne and Fonda have had little difficulty finding big roles in one genre: the Western, which has become increasingly preoccupied with aging heroes. During this period, the traditional romantic figure of the noble Westerner has been decisively abandoned, and Fonda, like his contemporaries, has found himself playing an assortment of comic non-heroes, derelicts, cowards, mercenaries, even crooks and brutal killers.

One of the most prolific directors of Westerns to emerge during the sixties was Burt Kennedy. In Kennedy's *The Rounders* (1965), a leisurely, low-key comedy set in the contemporary West, Fonda and Glenn Ford play itinerant horse wranglers who want to get out of debt. The aging, seedy, somewhat simple-minded cowpokes develop a grudging affection for a stubbornly wild horse, which they enter in a rodeo. This brings them some money, but the horse demolishes a

THE DIRTY GAME (1966). With Peter Van Eyck (right)

*SEX AND THE SINGLE GIRL (1964). As Frank*

barn, and, after paying for the damage, the men are as broke as ever.

The actors make a delightfully dry pair of non-heroes, with Fonda—drawling, befuddled and easy-going—a foil for the more explosive Ford. The film's highlights are Fonda's dancing the twist and their midnight swim with two Las Vegas strippers in a state fish hatchery, followed by an escape (in the nude) from a game warden.

Another comedy-Western, Fielder Cook's *A Big Hand for the Little Lady* (1966), abandons the wide open spaces for the back room of a saloon, where the territory's five richest men conduct their annual poker game. A passing hick (Fonda), who's promised his wife (Joanne Woodward) to give up poker, gets into the game, and invests their entire life's savings. He finally gets a good hand, but doesn't have enough money to stay in, and his anxiety leads to a heart attack. The wife, who knows nothing about cards, decides to continue; just by showing the hand to the town banker (Paul Ford), she gets enough of a loan to force the others out. At the end, we discover that it's all an elaborate trick, with Fonda and Woodward a pair of con artists employed by the banker.

The movie is basically a labored joke with a delayed punchline, but it amusingly controverts the traditional Western's assumptions about the nobility of women and the integrity of farmers. The latter, of course, is a Fonda staple, and Cook neatly uses his Honest Hank image to fool us. But Fonda isn't content merely to rely on this; he gives a genuinely creative performance, convincing us that he's a simpleton and a sucker (Hoppsy Pike in the Old West), and a whining, henpecked husband. When he's losing, and he effects a brave smile that doesn't conceal his nervousness, and when—right before the "attack"—he pleads desperately with the men to let him continue playing, we believe that we're watching someone who's hopelessly, pathetically addicted to gambling.

Fonda's most bizarre Western may be *Welcome to Hard Times* (1967), an allegory of the conflicts between good and evil, civilization and anarchic violence, restrained and aggressive sexuality, on the frontier. Hard Times is a tiny, ugly settlement, whose fifty inhabitants are terrorized by an evil stranger, The Man from Bodie (Aldo Ray). Without a word, he murders several people, rapes the dance-hall girl (Janice Rule), and burns the entire town. The unofficial mayor, a decent but ineffectual man (Fonda), together with a few others, rebuilds the community. They survive a bitter winter, during which Rule continually taunts Fonda about his cowardice in dealing with Ray. Inevitably the stranger returns to resume his reign of terror, and this time Fonda guns him down.

Writer-director Burt Kennedy, in a darker mood than in *The Rounders*, provides another anti-Western, not only in the drab setting (the antithesis of Ford's romantic frontier towns) but in Fonda's anti-heroic character. Although Fonda is again gentle and honest, his nonviolence stems from cowardice; although he's again building civilization, it's not out of a sense of history or adventure but because he's been running all his life and needs to regain confidence. And although he stands up to Ray, he's not the traditional Fonda character who realizes his responsibility or develops a sense of honor. His instinct is purely to survive, and he wins through trickery and accident, not courage. Fonda—and with him the Westerner—has lost his nobility.

At the beginning of *Stranger on the Run* (1967), Fonda—an aging, drunken derelict with torn clothing, a stubble, and a lost puppydog visage—looks seedier and more pathetic than ever. Thrown off a train, he finds himself in a small, burned-out town (the same set used in *Hard Times*), which was destroyed by ranchers angry at the railroad. To prevent further trouble, the railroad has hired as depu-

THE ROUNDERS (1965). As Howdy

ties a large number of killers, who are restless, hot tempered, and anxious for a fight. When a prostitute is murdered, Fonda is a convenient scapegoat, and the deputies, led by moody Michael Parks, go after him.

Since Fonda is on foot, they quickly overtake him, but Parks—wanting to make it more of a game—lets him go, and the pursuit resumes. This cat-and-mouse chase occupies much of the film, with Parks becoming increasingly angry and Fonda moving from whiny despair and weary resignation to growing strength and finally to a determination to stand up to Parks (an evolution beautifully imparted by Fonda's delicate performance).

Shot for television in only sixteen days, the film is far better than the average small-screen quickie, largely because of Don Siegel's sensitive direction. Siegel, on the threshold of major accomplishments (*Madigan*, *Dirty Harry*), captures a mood of futility, frustration and loneliness; as Andrew Sarris has said, "Siegel's most successful films express the doomed peculiarity of the antisocial outcast."*

In *Firecreek* (1968), the situation of *Welcome to Hard Times* is some-

*Andrew Sarris, *The American Cinema*, E. P. Dutton, p. 137

A BIG HAND FOR THE LITTLE LADY (1966). With Joanne Woodward

WELCOME TO HARD TIMES (1967). With Michael Shea

what reversed, with Fonda as an aging gunman whose gang threatens a tiny, frightened town. At first he opposes his men's terrorism, but, disabled by a wound, he is powerless to stop them. Later he joins them in hanging a deputy who has murdered a gang member. The formerly timid sheriff (James Stewart), really just a farmer, becames enraged, and boldly challenges the intruders. Fonda, reluctant to kill Stewart, shoots him in the leg to "slow him down," threatens to burn down the town if Stewart persists, and pleads with him to give up.

The stranger and the sheriff are archetypes conscious of their archetypal roles—unwilling to play them out to the inevitable conclusion, but aware that they must. Fonda, in particular, realizes that he's driven by the necessity of fulfilling an image, that of the individualistic gunfighter and natural leader, unable to conform to the rules of an emerging civilization. His leadership is eroding and his era is ending, but he continues to cling to a romanticized past, performing a part as if he had no free will.

Unfortunately, they are less characters than symbols; while this might fit into a more stylized context (a Sergio Leone film, for ex-

STRANGER ON THE RUN (1967). As the Stranger

FIRECREEK (1968). With James Stewart

ample), it doesn't work here. In the showdown, the inexperienced Stewart logically shouldn't stand a chance, but Fonda—representing a precivilized morality—must die. Therefore the script has him suddenly killed by a woman he's befriended, and her motivations are so cloudy that she functions simply as a *deus ex machina*. Still, Fonda's controlled, introverted emotion, his worn, unshaven appearance, and his look of desperation and resignation have rarely been used as expressively. And the film is interesting as the first occasion on which he's played so unregenerate a villain.

This was also the first joint appearance of the two friends since *A Miracle Can Happen*. (In *How the West Was Won* they played in separate segments.) In 1970 they teamed again for *The Cheyenne Social Club*, as seedy, nonheroic, affable cowboys of the 1870s. When Stewart inherits a business, he immediately heads for Cheyenne, and Fonda trails along; he's been following Stewart for ten years, though neither knows why. The business turns out to be a brothel, which surprises and upsets the upright Stewart, who wants to close it down, but delights Fonda, who works his way from one gold-hearted whore to another with the wide-eyed wonder of an adolescent.

It's a strangely harmonious combination: the moralistic, awkward stutterer and the libidinous, easygoing drawler. Director Gene Kelly's one-joke film gains resonance from the actors' genuine camaraderie, as they get drunk and sing together, argue politics (naturally Fonda is a Democrat, Stewart a Republican), and quarrel like a married couple. As with other male friendship films, the homosexual implications remain in the closet.

Fonda is constantly captivating. The opposite of the silent cowboy, he's so garrulous that he tells Stewart a nonstop story over their entire thousand-mile journey. He sings the theme song, which expresses a traditional Fonda aspiration ("Rollin' on just like a rollin' stone—lookin' for some land to call my own"); reacts with stupefied, open-mouthed expressions at their new life-style; and has some beautifully timed double-takes, especially his dazed realization that he's inadvertently caused a man's death during a showdown by cracking a pecan and thus distracting him.

*There Was a Crooked Man* (1970), set in Arizona in 1883, stars Fonda as a brave, incorruptible sheriff with a civilized aversion to violence, who becomes a prison warden. He determines to try out his liberal ideas of prison reform on

THE CHEYENNE SOCIAL CLUB (1970). With James Stewart

THERE WAS A CROOKED MAN (1970). With Kirk Douglas

a motley group of convicts, including one (Kirk Douglas) who's stolen and hidden $500,000. The men go along with Fonda's patient efforts at rehabilitation, all the while planning to stab, shoot and dynamite their way to freedom.

After the prison break, Douglas, in trying to recover his loot, is fatally bitten by a snake. Fonda finds the body, grabs the money and keeps riding. His idealism shattered by the escape, he feels that since nobody appreciated his honesty, he may as well be "crooked." As the title song sardonically suggests, "There's a little bit of bad in every good man."

This enchanting, low-key fable is sparked by the actors' easy manner—Fonda playing straight man to Douglas' charming scoundrel —and a witty script by Rober Benton and David Newman *(Bonnie and Clyde)* that effectivel satirizes Western movie myths Underlying the comedy is a cynicism characteristic of directo Joseph L. Mankiewicz *(All Abou Eve),* though this is probably hi most nihilistic work. Like *A Bi Hand for the Little Lady,* it cleverl exploits expectations created b Fonda's persona, but here he reall *is* an honest man who descends int corruption. The image is destroye —not merely reversed—and th implication is that liberalism an integrity are no longer viable. No incidentally, the film reflects Amer ica at the end of the cataclysmi sixties.

Previously, Fonda's image ha undergone its most complete devas

ONCE UPON A TIME IN THE WEST (1969). As Frank

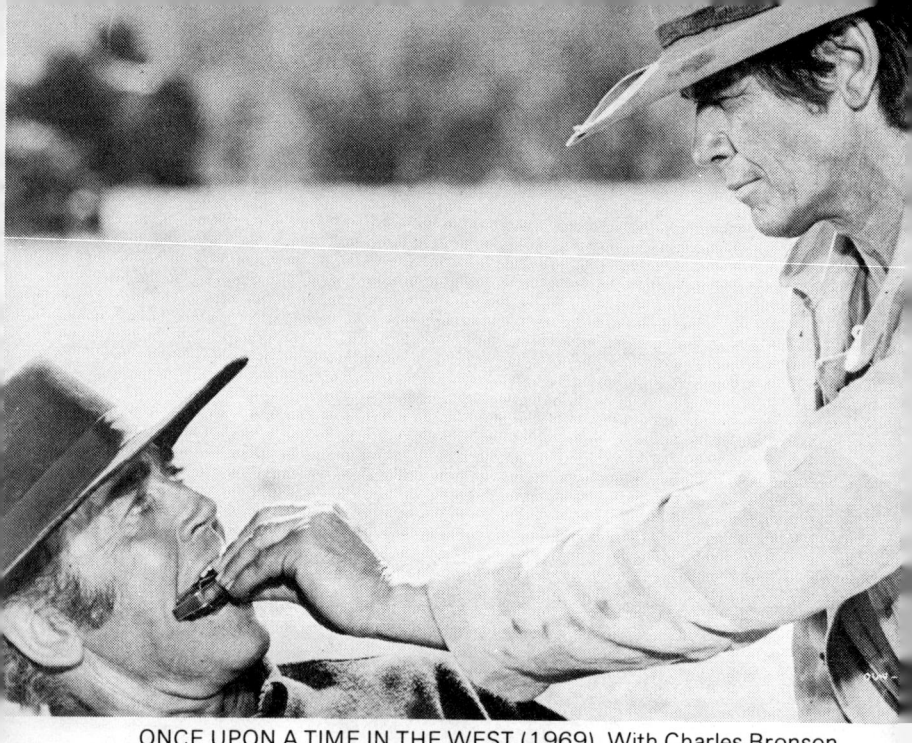

ONCE UPON A TIME IN THE WEST (1969). With Charles Bronson

tation in Sergio Leone's *Once Upon a Time in the West* (1969). Leone, whose Italian Westerns with Clint Eastwood had been hugely successful (and widely imitated), was given $5,000,000 and complete freedom for this epic, and the result was a highly personal tribute to the West and the Western. Although it was a big hit in Europe, it was a disaster in the United States, probably because its slow pace discouraged action fans. Nonetheless, it is magnificent in conception and execution, and is probably Fonda's best non-Ford Western.

The ornately complex plot concerns the coming of the railroad in the 1870s and the attempts by a ruthless railroad baron to grab up all valuable land. The characters include Frank (Fonda), the baron's hired gunman; Jill (Claudia Cardinale), whose land the railroad covets; and the enigmatic Man with the Harmonica (Charles Bronson), who is planning revenge on Frank for the murder of his brother. In Leone's atmosphere of myth and eulogy, they are elevated to archetypes—the old gunfighter, the earth-mother to an emerging civilization, and the agent of destiny, respectively—with the men particularly conscious of their mythic roles.

This grand design is supported by Leone's baroque style: his brilliant use of the wide screen, alternating between panoramas of desolate but strangely beautiful landscapes and huge close-ups of faces that *become* landscapes, or between static shots and exquisitely choreographed camera movements; his unique way of extending every event, a kind of operatic neorealism in which each gesture and detail takes on cosmic significance; his use of Ennio Morricone's majestic score; his incorporation of John Ford's Monument Valley, with all of its mythic reverberations.

Fonda's first appearance is singularly chilling. A man, his daughter (a vision of innocence in white) and his son prepare a meal outdoors: a feeling of peace, purity and harmony with nature is established. Suddenly, the father and daughter are murdered, and the five killers emerge. Their leader has a familiar walk, but we're not certain until he approaches the little boy, and the camera, behind him in close-up, circles around and stares into the icy blue eyes of Henry Fonda. The symbol of decency smiles reassuringly at the child, spits out tobacco, and calmly guns him down.

Fonda says that he tried to change his looks for this role with

MY NAME IS NOBODY (1974). With Terence Hill

MADIGAN (1968). With James Whitmore and Richard Widmark

brown contact lenses and a villainous mustache. But when he arrived on the set, "looking sinister as hell," Leone told him to remove the disguise. This made Fonda feel that Leone cast him mainly for the shock of his first scene: "He wanted the baby blues—he wanted the Fonda face . . . to make the audience for that one scene, say, 'Jesus Christ, it's Henry Fonda!' "

Of course Fonda enlarges on the opening characterization—shooting men point-blank ("People scare best when they're dyin'."), kidnapping and raping Cardinale, letting his crippled boss struggle and die in the mud. Films like *Warlock* and *Firecreek* prepared us for Fonda the killer, and there was something calculating and potentially violent in even his earliest characters. But never was he so thorough an embodiment of evil.

Part of the horror derives from our realization that Fonda now works for the railroad—the symbol of corporation ruthlessness mercilessly destroying people in its path—that was his enemy in films like *Jesse James*. Actually, Leone's attitude is complex: when the train finally reaches Jill's land, it becomes a stirring symbol of progress and civilization; the real enemy may not be the railroad, but the men who run it. To an extent even Frank is a victim—the romantic, individualistic gunman exploited by impersonal capitalism—though at the end we learn that he was sadistic even when young.

This is revealed during his showdown with the Man, when the latter remembers that as a boy, he was forced by Frank to participate in his own brother's hanging. The memory flashback (in which Fonda, amazingly, looks to be in his thirties) is intercut with the present, where the men move ritualistically toward each other. There's an overwhelming sense of the past controlling events and individuals; like a Lang character, Frank has been doomed from the start. As he dies, with a shocked recognition of the Man's identity, Frank suddenly becomes a pathetic pawn of fate.

Because Fonda enjoyed this role, he agreed to do *My Name is Nobody* (1974), directed by Tonino Valerii and based on a Leone idea. Valerii had been Leone's assistant, and the influence is obvious in the portentous close-ups, the lyrically choreographed action, the drawing out of events, the Morricone music. Like *Once Upon a Time in the West*, it's about legends and myths, and the end of the Old West. (The year, 1899, is obviously significant.) Here the theme emerges in self-conscious discussions rather than through actions, but it's still a diverting fable.

Fonda, as Jack Beauregard, the fastest gun alive, again kills casually, but this time all of his victims were out to get him first, and he's just a nice guy who wants to be left alone. At fifty-one (Fonda, though sixty-eight, really seems to be in his fifties), he's tired of having to prove his skill, and wants to retire into anonymity by going to Europe. But along comes "Nobody" (Terence Hill), Leone's nameless agent of destiny—a young, equally fast gunman who idolizes Jack and keeps telling him that he has to go out in style by realizing the potential of his legend.

"Nobody" wants Jack to face the entire 150-member Wild Bunch, a showdown he manages to arrange, despite Jack's reluctance. ("My only destiny is to get the hell out of here.") Jack succeeds in insuring his legend (underlined by slow-motion shots of the Bunch dying and freeze frames of the action as part of a history book). Now the only way he can quit is to die, so he and Nobody fake a gunfight in which Jack is "killed."

Fonda ideally embodies the slightly melancholy, stoic man of action at the end of his career, and the individual predestined by his own myth. His dry humor and bemused irony perfectly offset Hill's agressive clowning. And the final scene is moving: over a shot of Jack's grave, his voice, addressing Nobody, discusses the New West, where no man can be trusted and survival outweighs nobility. Since we don't yet know that the gunfight was faked, the effect is like that of *Mister*

THE BOSTON STRANGLER (1968). With Tony Curtis

*Roberts'* ending: a dead man inspiring the individual who will carry on his tradition. But now the message is not one of heroism; it's an epitaph for courage, and a farewell to the romantic Old West, reinforced by the revelation that Jack is sneaking out of the country.

Like the modern Western, the urban police thriller, which often recasts the conflicts of the frontier in contemporary molds, has had its traditional good-evil distinctions replaced by moral uncertainties. *Madigan* (1968), which reunited Fonda and Don Siegel, did have a vicious, psychotic killer. But it also viewed certain lawmen with misgivings: the New York City police commissioner, Anthony Russell (Fonda), is proud of his incorruptibility and his strict enforcement of the letter of the law, but he thinks nothing of having a married mistress (Susan Clark); and his chief inspector and oldest friend, Charles Kane (James Whitmore) has accepted a bribe.

Ordinarily, Russell's unyielding severity toward Kane might at least make us admire him as an honest cop, but in the film's moral scheme, corruption is preferable to self-righteousness. Russell's lack of compassion is also revealed in his harshness toward Detective Madigan (Richard Widmark), who has allowed a killer to escape, and whom he angrily gives seventy-two hours to bring in the man. Siegel, as in his subsequent police movies *Coogan's Bluff* and *Dirty Harry*, expresses a romantic attitude toward the individualist cop at odds with the higher echelons.

Besides his problems with Kane and Madigan, Russell is worried because his mistress wants to end their relationship, and because a black minister is alleging that his son was subjected to police brutality. Consequently, his mind always seems to be elsewhere. Fonda adeptly conveys this distracted manner, and he flows through the film with his usual grace. But his is a lightly sketched character; Siegel continually abandons Russell's problems for scenes of the manhunt (filmed with his distinctive flair for pacing), and the emphasis is really on Madigan.

Fonda is among Siegel's admirers, but he was disappointed in his role. He had been attracted to the project because of the book, the different emphasis of which is obvious from its title, *The Commissioner*. According to Fonda, the producer or the studio insisted on shifting the focus to the action: "That was fine, but all of us, including Widmark, felt that the picture would have been better if there had been more depth to the commissioner."

Another crime movie, *The Boston Strangler* (1968), which depicts the search for the man who terrorized Boston between 1962 and 1964, is, despite its psychological and sociological pretensions, just a slick thriller. Fonda is dignified as Bottomly, the brooding, intellectual assistant attorney general assigned to coordinate the investigation. At first reluctant, he becomes dedicated to his unpleasant task, in which he's aided by a tough detective (George Kennedy). When Albert De Salvo (Tony Curtis) is arrested, Bottomly questions him endlessly, with a quiet, persistent determination. Success comes when De Salvo, observed through a two-way mirror, almost strangles his wife. Although this isn't enough evidence to prove De Salvo's guilt, Bottomly is certain that he has his man.

Perhaps because *Spencer's Mountain*, unlike many of his other sixties films, had been immensely successful, Fonda was again cast as the head of a huge family in *Yours, Mine and Ours* (1968). The result was one of his biggest hits ever. The film depicts the psychological and logistical problems that result when a widower (Fonda) with ten children marries a widow (Lucille Ball) with eight children. She even be-

YOURS, MINE AND OURS (1968). With Lucille Ball

comes pregnant again, but what's one more child when you already have eighteen?

Director Melville Shavelson based his script on a real California family, but it's still a tired, television-style situation comedy. And although Fonda walks through the film with ease, his character—a navy officer who runs the family like a military organization ("Mutiny was simply not tolerated")—is somewhat offensive.

Like *Spencer's Mountain*, the film is filled with sly, sexual innuendoes, while affirming enough Middle American values to make it

a Silent Majority favorite. Nowhere are the realities of 1968 in evidence. The oldest son is drafted, but there's no anxiety about—or even reference to—Vietnam. Fonda tells his daughter that sex is only for having babies, which indicates the film's primitive attitude at a time of exploding populations.

A few years later, he played a conservative character in a *real* television situation comedy, "The Smith Family." This half-hour ABC series, which began in January, 1971 and was immediately renewed for a second season, starred Fonda as a plainclothes police sergeant, happily married and the father of three children who love cops. At the time, Fonda, explaining why he had agreed to do a second television series, said that he wanted to show that cops could be nice guys: "I'm for law and order, and cops take a bad rap from kids today. I don't think policemen should be put down because of a few bad officers any more than all college kids should be put down because of what happens on campuses."

To Fonda's credit, he insisted on rejecting scripts, fought with the producers and writers, and later regretted having done this embarrassing series. But his main objection was that it became too much like "Ozzie and Harriet;" the politics didn't bother him. Fonda still considered himself a liberal and supported men like McGovern. But the Midwestern liberalism of the thirties was a far cry from the positions taken by Jane Fonda and other radicals in the sixties and seventies.

In *Sometimes a Great Notion* (1971), based on Ken Kesey's novel of a contemporary lumberjacking family that stubbornly maintains nineteenth-century frontier values, Fonda plays his most reactionary character. Henry Stamper, the crusty patriarch, is a staunch advocate of hard work and rugged individualism. He derides his younger son Lee (Michael Sarrazin) for his college education and long hair, is proud of his social apathy, and says that his purpose in life is "to work and eat and sleep and screw and drink and to keep on goin'—that's all there is."

Henry exerts an authoritarian influence over his older son Hank (Paul Newman, who also directed), his nephew Joe (Richard Jaeckel), and their families. When the other lumberjacks strike, the Stampers alienate the entire community by continuing to work: they have a contract to honor and are against "pinko" unions. They overcome hostility, sabotage and violence, but are thwarted by nature, when a falling log drowns Joe and kills Henry by severing his arm.

Grizzled, foul-mouthed and looking his age for a change, Fonda is extremely colorful. Our amusement (and our discomfort) derive from the irony that quasi-revolutionary Tom Joad has become intransigently anti-union three decades later. Stamper is like Fonda's early characters in his rural individualism, opposition to progress, and adherence to the principles that built the country. The difference is that he's now in the twentieth century, where his individualism affects others adversely.

Occasionally the film recognizes this negative side and makes the Stampers seem just plain ornery. But they're largely appealing and heroic, and the ending is unmistak-

SOMETIMES A GREAT NOTION (1971). As Henry Stamper

able in its celebration of their rugged courage. Despite the many setbacks, Hank and Lee decide to finish the job of floating the logs downstream. As the strikers watch in anger, Hank, emphasizing his defiance, ties Henry's arm to the tugboat, with its middle finger extended in the familiar gesture of contempt. In *Mister Roberts* the hero lived on through his inspiring letter; here Fonda's influence also continues posthumously, but it's the most grotesque apotheosis of the actor's career.

His remaining films of the early seventies were less exciting. In *The Alpha Caper* (1973), a television movie, he played a parole officer, embittered by forced retirement, who embarks on a crime along with three of his parolees. Fonda was also in *The Serpent* (1973), a complicated French throwback to the Cold War spy melodramas of the fifties and sixties. Here he was cast as the tough but good-natured head of the CIA, which is questioning a defecting Russian secret police colonel (Yul Brynner) in an attempt to discover the names of enemy agents. The film was barely released in the United States.

He was teamed for the first time with Elizabeth Taylor in *Ash Wednesday* (1973), but his role is small, and is restricted to the latter part of the film. A wealthy lawyer, he is bored with his thirty-year marriage to a formerly beautiful woman (Taylor), now in her fifties. She believes that her faded appearance is to blame, and heads for an Italian clinic, where she undergoes a plastic surgery process that rejuvenates her entire body as well as her face. When Fonda arrives, and sees the miraculously transformed woman, he feels guilty about her ordeal, but still isn't interested. She tries to recapture the excitement of their honeymoon, but to no avail.

Fonda's greatest satisfaction since the late sixties has again been the theater. In 1968 he joined the Plumstead Playhouse, a group which hoped eventually to establish an American repertory company, and whose members included Robert Ryan, Martha Scott, Mildred Natwick, and Ed Begley. For their first season, in the fall of 1968, they did two productions in Mineola, New York: Hecht and MacArthur's *The Front Page*, in which Fonda played a tiny role as a reporter (and received excellent notices) and Thornton Wilder's *Our Town*, starring Fonda as the Stage Manager.

The actor loves *Our Town* and thinks it deserves to be revived as often as possible. Of course his role, with its Middle American folk wisdom, was perfect for him. Clive Barnes said that Fonda "might have been born to play the Stage Manager . . . (he has) to perfection that

ASH WEDNESDAY (1973). With Elizabeth Taylor

homespun elegance and dignity the part requires." In November 1969 he returned to Broadway for another Plumstead production of *Our Town*—a limited run of thirty-six performances—and in March 1970 he directed and starred in a Los Angeles production.

In 1970 Fonda also toured in a one-man show, *Fathers Against Sons Against Fathers*. He read and performed passages dealing with the generation gap, by Shakespeare, Steinbeck, Ben Franklin, Arthur Miller, Bob Dylan, and others. In 1971 Fonda directed, but did not appear in, *The Caine Mutiny Court-Martial* in Los Angeles, and in early 1972 he went on national tour with William Saroyan's *The Time of Your Life*.

But the major event of his recent stage career has been *Clarence Darrow*, a one-man show by David W. Rintels, in which Fonda narrated highlights of the criminal lawyer's life and enacted parts of his famous trials. Fonda has said, "All I knew about Darrow was that he defended Leopold-Loeb and was in the Scopes monkey trial. So I went back and researched like I never remember doing for another part." As a result, he "fell in love" with Darrow. Fonda obviously connected with Darrow's Midwestern liberalism and his concern for the underdog. In many respects the character, and Fonda's performance, were reminiscent of *Young Mr. Lincoln*.

Although he didn't attempt completely to impersonate Darrow, Fonda did use spectacles, rumpled clothing, a lock of straight hair for the "hayseed" look, and padding to simulate a paunch. It was a tour de force: Fonda, onstage alone for almost two hours, addressing imaginary judges, juries and witnesses as well as the audience; moving deftly from rustic humor to impassioned oratory. In *The New York Times*, Walter Kerr observed, "A subliminal Darrow usurps the Fonda personality, and the game is not won by charm or easy skill but by intellectual metamorphosis. I think the actor has *thought* his way freshly through the problems without precedent that once beset Darrow . . . and in the thinking arrived at a magical sleight-of-mind. The performance is perfect."

The play, which opened on Broadway on March 24, 1974, was scheduled for a five-week run. But on April 23, four days before closing night, Fonda, exhausted from the grueling role, collapsed backstage after his performance. He had to have a pacemaker permanently implanted in his chest, and the rest of the run as well as performances in other cities were canceled. But he went through with a Los Angeles engagement in the summer, and

As Clarence Darrow (on television, September 4, 1974)

On the set of CAT BALLOU (1965) with daughter Jane

did a ninety-minute television version in September—another superb performance, which reconfirmed his command of every medium.

In 1975, Fonda celebrated his seventieth birthday and his fortieth year in films. Despite his health problems he showed little sign of slowing down. Early in the year, in fact, he resumed his tour of *Clarence Darrow*, which included a return engagement on Broadway.

His children, of course, have become heroic figures to younger Americans. Peter's "Captain America" in *Easy Rider* was the ideal rebel for the late sixties, just as Henry's Tom Joad had been for the early forties. For her acting talents, Jane has received deserved acclaim, including the Academy Award (for *Klute*) that has eluded her father. Jane's activities in political areas have led to condemnation from Middle America, but many people respect her, and no one can seriously accuse her of insincerity.

For years, the press continually ran stories about Henry's conflicts with his offspring over their lifestyles, but the disagreements seem to be over; Fonda even admires his daughter's husband, activist Tom Hayden, and says that Darrow would probably have defended the Chicago Seven (of which Hayden was one). As of this writing, the three Fondas are planning to unite professionally for the first time. They would play an average American family during the Revolutionary War, in a film to be released as part of the nation's bicentennial celebration.

Whether or not this comes to fruition, it is certainly a fitting idea for Henry Fonda, who once again would be back at the birth of the country, the mythic pioneer hero building America. During the past decade, his characters have deviated considerably from the transcendent goodness of his previous Revolutionary hero in *Drums Along the Mohawk*, far from the honest simplicity of Abe Lincoln, far from the ingenuousness of Hoppsy Pike. But even after his transformation into thoroughly malevolent villains, as in *Once Upon a Time in the West*, his fundamental image has remained indestructible.

His triumph in *Clarence Darrow* is conclusive proof that this also continues to extend to theater and television. Standing alone on the stage, a single spotlight shining on his honest Midwestern face, he still has the power to move us, to inspire complete trust. Through four decades, he has endured as the quintessential man of integrity.

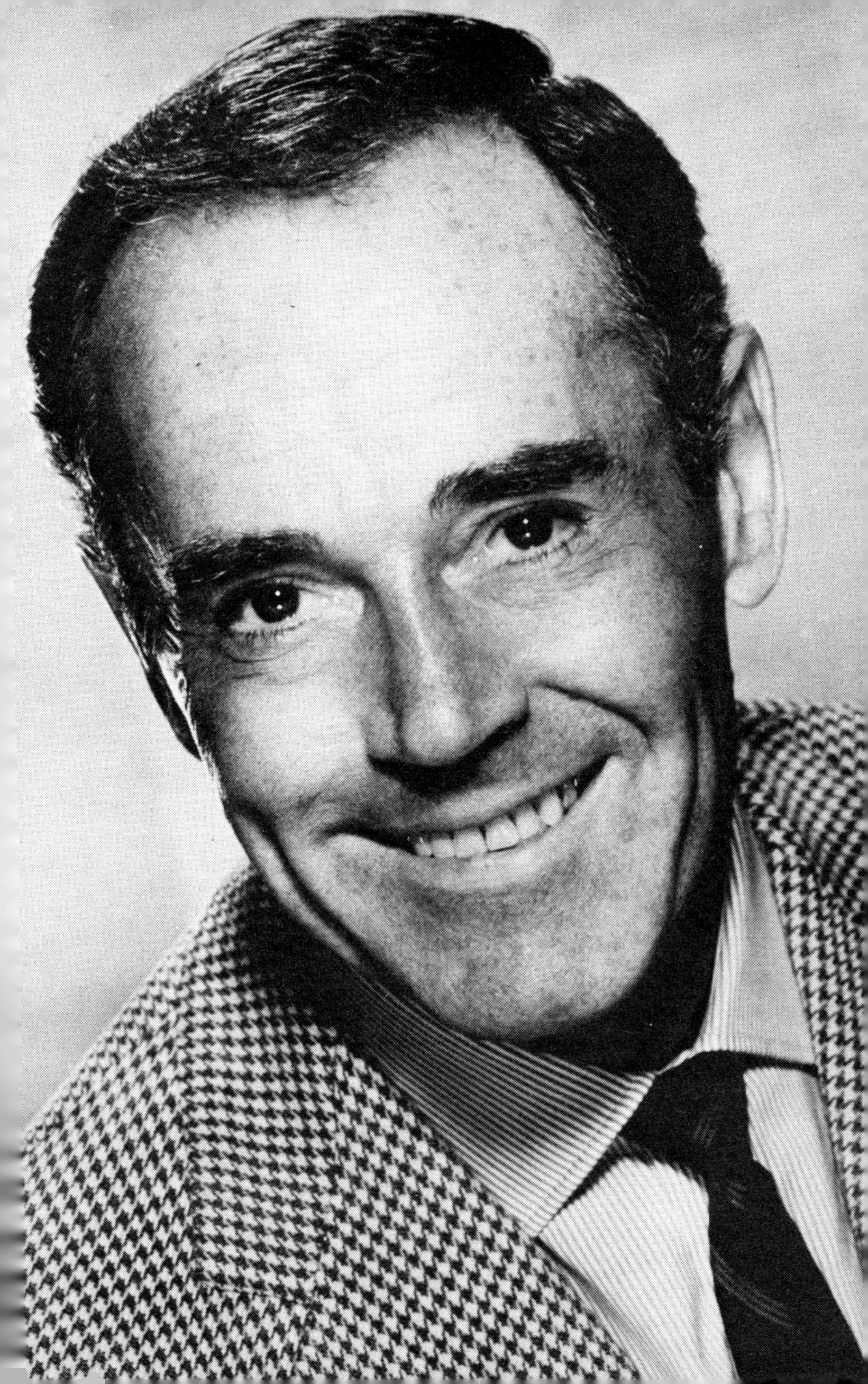

# BIBLIOGRAPHY

Agee, James. *Agee on Film*. Boston: Beacon Press, 1958.
Anderson, Lindsay. "John Ford." *Cinema*, Spring 1971. (written in 1955)
Bogdanovich, Peter. "Homage to Hank." *The New York Times*, July 3, 1966.
―――. *Fritz Lang in America*. New York: Praeger, 1969.
―――. *John Ford*. Berkeley: University of California Press, 1968.
Bowser, Eileen (ed.). *Film Notes*. New York: The Museum of Modern Art, 1969.
Brough, James. *The Fabulous Fondas*. New York: David McKay, 1973.
Corliss, Richard. *Talking Pictures*. New York: Overlook, 1974.
Cowie, Peter. *Seventy Years of Cinema*. New York: A.S. Barnes, 1969.
Fonda, Henry (interview). *Dialogue on Film*. Beverly Hills: The American Film Institute, November 1973.
Fonda, Henry (Career Checklist). *Monthly Film Bulletin*. British Film Institute. April 1968.
Gussow, Mel. *Don't Say Yes Until I Finish Talking*. New York: Doubleday, 1971.
Jameson, Richard T. "Something To Do With Death." *Film Comment*, March-April, 1973.
Kaminsky, Stuart M. *Don Siegel: Director*. New York: Curtis Books, 1974.
Lawson, John Howard. *Film: The Creative Process*. New York: Hill & Wang, 1964.
Sarris, Andrew. *The American Cinema*. New York: E.P. Dutton, 1968.
―――. *Confessions of a Cultist*. New York: Simon & Schuster, 1971.
―――. *The Primal Screen*. New York: Simon & Schuster, 1973.
Schickel, Richard. *The Stars*. New York: Bonanza, 1962.
Sennett, Ted. *Lunatics and Lovers*. New Rochelle: Arlington House, 1974.
Smith, Ella. *Starring Miss Barbara Stanwyck*. New York: Crown Publishers, 1974.
Springer, John. *The Fondas*. New York: Citadel Press, 1970.
Steinbeck, John. *The Grapes of Wrath*. New York: Viking, 1939.
Thompson, Thomas. "Fonda at 68 . . . 68?" *McCall's*, September 1973.
Truffaut, François. *Hitchcock*. New York: Simon & Schuster, 1967.
Vidor, King. *King Vidor on Filmmaking*. New York: David McKay, 1972.
Walker, Alexander. *Stardom—The Hollywood Phenomenon*. New York: Stein & Day, 1970.
Wood, Robin. *Hitchcock's Films*. New York: A.S. Barnes, 1965.

# THE FILMS OF HENRY FONDA

The director's name follows the release date. A (c) following the release date indicates that the film is in color. Sp indicates Screenplay and b/o indicates based/on.

1. THE FARMER TAKES A WIFE. Fox, 1935. *Victor Fleming*. Sp: Edwin Burke, b/o play by Frank B. Elser and Marc Connelly. Cast: Janet Gaynor, Charles Bickford, Slim Summerville, Andy Devine, Roger Imhof, Jane Withers, Margaret Hamilton. Remade as a musical in 1953.

2. WAY DOWN EAST. Fox, 1935. *Henry King*. Sp: Howard Estabrook and William Hurlbut, b/o play by Lottie Blair Parker. Cast: Rochelle Hudson, Slim Summerville, Edward Trevor, Margaret Hamilton, Andy Devine, Russell Simpson, Spring Byington. Previously filmed in 1920.

3. I DREAM TOO MUCH. RKO-Radio, 1935. *John Cromwell*. Sp: James Gow and Edmund North, b/o story by Elsie Finn and David G. Wittels. Cast: Lily Pons, Eric Blore, Osgood Perkins, Lucien Littlefield, Esther Dale, Lucille Ball.

4. THE TRAIL OF THE LONESOME PINE. Paramount, 1936. (c) *Henry Hathaway*. Sp: Grover Jones, Harvey Thew and Horace McCoy, b/o novel by John Fox, Jr. Cast: Sylvia Sidney, Fred MacMurray, Fred Stone, Fuzzy Knight, Beulah Bondi, Robert Barrat, Spanky McFarland. Previously filmed in 1916 and 1923.

5. THE MOON'S OUR HOME. Paramount, 1936. *William A. Seiter*. Sp: Isabel Dawn, Boyce DeGaw, Dorothy Parker and Alan Campbell, b/o novel by Faith Baldwin. Cast: Margaret Sullavan, Charles Butterworth, Beulah Bondi, Margaret Hamilton, Walter Brennan, Henrietta Crosman.

6. SPENDTHRIFT. Paramount, 1936. *Raoul Walsh*. Sp: Raoul Walsh and Bert Hanlon, b/o story by Eric Hatch. Cast: Pat Paterson, Mary Brian, June Brewster, George Barbier, Halliwell Hobbes.

7. WINGS OF THE MORNING. 20th Century-Fox, 1937. (c) *Harold Schuster*. Sp: Tom Geraghty, b/o stories by Donn Byrne. Cast: Annabella, Leslie Banks, Stewart Rome, John McCormack.

8. YOU ONLY LIVE ONCE. A Walter Wanger Production, released by United Artists, 1937. *Fritz Lang*. Sp: Gene Towne and Graham Baker. Cast: Sylvia Sidney, Barton MacLane, Jean Dixon, William Gargan, Jerome Cowan, Chic Sale, Margaret Hamilton.

9. SLIM. Warner Brothers, 1937. *Ray Enright*. Sp: William Wister Haines, b/o his novel. Cast: Pat O'Brien, Margaret Lindsay, Stuart Erwin, J. Farrell MacDonald, Dick Purcell, Joseph Sawyer.

10. THAT CERTAIN WOMAN. Warner Brothers, 1937. *Edmund Goulding*. Sp: Edmund Goulding. Cast: Bette Davis, Ian Hunter, Donald Crisp, Anita Louise, Hugh O'Connell, Katherine Alexander. A remake of *The Trespasser* (1929).

11. I MET MY LOVE AGAIN. A Walter Wanger Production, released by United Artists, 1938. *Arthur Ripley* and *Joshua Logan*. Sp: David Hertz, b/o novel *Summer Lightning* by Allene Corliss. Cast: Joan Bennett, Dame May Whitty, Alan Marshal, Louise Platt, Alan Baxter, Tim Holt.

12. JEZEBEL. Warner Brothers, 1938. *William Wyler*. Sp: Clements Ripley, Abem Finkel and John Huston, b/o play by Owen Davis. Cast: Bette Davis, George Brent, Margaret Lindsay, Fay Bainter, Donald Crisp, Richard Cromwell, Henry O'Neill, Spring Byington.

13. BLOCKADE. A Walter Wanger Production, released by United Artists, 1938. *William Dieterle*. Sp: John Howard Lawson. Cast: Madeleine Carroll, Leo Carrillo, John Halliday, Vladimir Sokoloff, Robert Warwick.

14. SPAWN OF THE NORTH. Paramount, 1938. *Henry Hathaway*. Sp: Jules Furthman, b/o novel by Barrett Willoughby. Cast: George Raft, Dorothy Lamour, Louise Platt, John Barrymore, Akim Tamiroff, Lynne Overman. Remade in 1954 as *Alaska Seas*.

15. THE MAD MISS MANTON. RKO-Radio, 1938. *Leigh Jason*. Sp: Philip G. Epstein, b/o story by Wilson Collinson. Cast: Barbara Stanwyck, Sam Levene, Frances Mercer, Stanley Ridges, Whitney Bourne.

16. JESSE JAMES. 20th Century-Fox, 1939. (c) *Henry King*. Sp: Nunnally Johnson. Cast: Tyrone Power, Nancy Kelly, Randolph Scott, Henry Hull, Slim Summerville, J. Edward Bromberg, Brian Donlevy, John Carradine, Donald Meek, Jane Darwell.

17. LET US LIVE. Columbia, 1939. *John Brahm*. Sp: Anthony Veiller and Allen Rivkin, b/o story by Joseph F. Dinneen. Cast: Maureen O'Sullivan, Ralph Bellamy, Alan Baxter, Stanley Ridges, Henry Kolker.

18. THE STORY OF ALEXANDER GRAHAM BELL. 20th Century-Fox, 1939. *Irving Cummings*. Sp: Lamar Trotti, b/o story by Ray Harris. Cast: Don Ameche, Loretta Young, Charles Coburn, Gene Lockhart, Spring Byington.

19. YOUNG MR. LINCOLN. 20th Century-Fox, 1939. *John Ford*. Sp: Lamar Trotti. Cast: Alice Brady, Marjorie Weaver, Arleen Whelan, Eddie Collins, Pauline Moore, Richard Cromwell, Donald Meek, Dorris Bowdon, Eddie Quillan, Ward Bond.

20. DRUMS ALONG THE MOHAWK. 20th Century-Fox, 1939. (c) *John Ford*. Sp: Lamar Trotti and Sonya Levien, b/o novel by Walter D. Edmonds. Cast: Claudette Colbert, Edna May Oliver, Eddie Collins, John Carradine, Dorris Bowdon, Jessie Ralph, Arthur Shields, Robert Lowery.

21. THE GRAPES OF WRATH. 20th Century-Fox, 1940. *John Ford*. Sp: Nunnally Johnson, b/o novel by John Steinbeck. Cast: Jane Darwell, John Carradine, Charley Grapewin, Dorris Bowdon, Russell Simpson, O.Z. Whitehead, John Qualen, Eddie Quillan.

22. LILLIAN RUSSELL. 20th Century-Fox, 1940. *Irving Cummings*. Sp: William Anthony McGuire. Cast: Alice Faye, Don Ameche, Edward Arnold, Warren William, Leo Carrillo, Helen Westley.

23. THE RETURN OF FRANK JAMES. 20th Century-Fox, 1940 (c). *Fritz Lang*. Sp: Sam Hellman. Cast: Gene Tierney, Jackie Cooper, Henry Hull, John Carradine, J. Edward Bromberg, Donald Meek, Eddie Collins.

24. CHAD HANNA. 20th Century-Fox, 1940 (c). *Henry King*. Sp: Nunnally Johnson, b/o story *Red Wheels Rolling* by Walter D. Edmonds. Cast: Dorothy Lamour, Linda Darnell, Guy Kibbee, Jane Darwell, John Carradine.

25. THE LADY EVE. Paramount, 1941. *Preston Sturges*. Sp: Preston Sturges, b/o story by Monckton Hoffe. Cast: Barbara Stanwyck, Charles Coburn, Eugene Pallette, William Demarest, Eric Blore, Melville Cooper. Remade in 1956 as *The Birds and the Bees*.

26. WILD GEESE CALLING. 20th Century-Fox, 1941. *John Brahm*. Sp: Horace McCoy, b/o novel by Stewart Edward White. Cast: Joan Bennett, Warren William, Ona Munson, Barton MacLane, Russell Simpson.

27. YOU BELONG TO ME. Columbia, 1941. *Wesley Ruggles*. Sp: Claude Binyon, b/o story by Dalton Trumbo. Cast: Barbara Stanwyck, Edgar Buchanan, Roger Clark, Ruth Donnelly, Melville Cooper. Remade in 1950 as *Emergency Wedding*.

28. THE MALE ANIMAL. Warner Brothers, 1942. *Elliott Nugent*. Sp: Julius J. and Philip G. Epstein and Stephen Morehouse Avery, b/o play by James Thurber and Elliott Nugent. Cast: Olivia de Havilland, Jack Carson, Joan Leslie, Eugene Pallette, Herbert Anderson. Remade in 1952 as *She's Working Her Way Through College*.

29. RINGS ON HER FINGERS. 20th Century-Fox, 1942. *Rouben Mamoulian*. Sp: Ken Englund, b/o story by Robert Pirosh and Joseph Schrank. Cast: Gene Tierney, Laird Cregar, John Sheppard, Henry Stephenson, Spring Byington.

30. THE MAGNIFICENT DOPE. 20th Century-Fox, 1942. *Walter Lang*. Sp: George Seaton, b/o story by Joseph Schrank. Cast: Lynn Bari, Don Ameche, Edward Everett Horton, George Barbier, Frank Orth.

31. TALES OF MANHATTAN. 20th Century-Fox, 1942. *Julien Duvivier*. Sp: Ben Hecht, Ferenc Molnar, Donald Ogden Stewart, Samuel Hoffenstein, Alan Campbell, Ladislas Fodor, L. Vadnai, L. Gorog, Lamar Trotti and Henry Blankfort. Cast: Charles Boyer, Rita Hayworth, Ginger Rogers, Charles Laughton, Edward G. Robinson, Paul Robeson, Ethel Waters, Eddie Anderson, Thomas Mitchell, Eugene Pallette, Cesar Romero.

32. THE BIG STREET. RKO-Radio, 1942. *Irving Reis*. Sp: Leonard Spigelgass, b/o story *Little Pinks* by Damon Runyon. Cast: Lucille Ball, Barton MacLane, Eugene Pallette, Agnes Moorehead, Sam Levene, Ray Collins.

33. THE OX-BOW INCIDENT. 20th Century-Fox, 1943. *William Wellman*. Sp: Lamar Trotti, b/o novel by Walter Van Tilburg Clark. Cast: Dana Andrews, Mary Beth Hughes, Anthony Quinn, William Eythe, Henry Morgan, Jane Darwell, Matt Briggs, Harry Davenport, Frank Conroy.

34. THE IMMORTAL SERGEANT. 20th Century-Fox, 1943. *John Stahl*. Sp: Lamar Trotti, b/o novel by John Brophy. Cast: Maureen O'Hara, Thomas Mitchell, Allyn Joslyn, Reginald Gardiner, Melville Cooper.

35. MY DARLING CLEMENTINE. 20th Century-Fox, 1946. *John Ford*. Sp: Samuel G. Engel and Winston Miller, b/o story by Sam Hellman, from book *Wyatt Earp, Frontier Marshal* by Stuart N. Lake. Cast: Linda Darnell, Victor Mature, Walter Brennan, Tim Holt, Ward Bond, Cathy Downs, Alan Mowbray, John Ireland, Grant Withers. A remake of *Frontier Marshal* (1939).

36. THE LONG NIGHT. RKO-Radio, 1947. *Anatole Litvak*. Sp: John Wexley, b/o story by Jacques Viot and Marcel Carné's film *Le Jour Se Leve (Daybreak)*. Cast: Barbara Bel Geddes, Vincent Price, Ann Dvorak, Moroni Olsen, Elisha Cook, Jr..

37. THE FUGITIVE. Argosy-RKO Radio, 1947. *John Ford*. Sp: Dudley Nichols, b/o novel *The Power and the Glory* (or *The Labyrinthine Ways*) by Graham Greene. Cast: Dolores Del Rio, Pedro Armendariz, Ward Bond, Leo Carrillo, J. Carrol Naish.

38. DAISY KENYON. 20th Century-Fox, 1947. *Otto Preminger*. Sp: David Hertz, b/o novel by Elizabeth Janeway. Cast: Joan Crawford, Dana Andrews, Ruth Warrick, Martha Stewart, Peggy Ann Garner.

39. A MIRACLE CAN HAPPEN (ON OUR MERRY WAY). A Bogeaus-Meredith Production released by United Artists, 1948. *King Vidor* and *Leslie Fenton* (and, uncredited, *George Stevens* and *John Huston*). Sp: Laurence Stallings, Lou Breslow, b/o story by Arch Oboler; Fonda-Stewart segment by John O'Hara. Cast: James Stewart, Burgess Meredith, Paulette Goddard, Fred MacMurray, Dorothy Lamour, Dorothy Ford, Harry James, Eduardo Ciannelli.

40. FORT APACHE. Argosy-RKO Radio, 1948. *John Ford*. Sp: Frank S. Nugent, b/o story *Massacre* by James Warner Bellah. Cast: John Wayne, Shirley Temple, John Agar, Ward Bond, George O'Brien, Victor McLaglen, Pedro Armendariz, Anna Lee.

41. JIGSAW. A Danzinger Production, released by United Artists, 1949. *Fletcher Markle*. Sp: Fletcher Markle and Vincent O'Connor, b/o story by John Roeburt. Cast: Franchot Tone, Jean Wallace, Myron McCormick, Marc Lawrence. Fonda appeared briefly, along with other stars.

42. MISTER ROBERTS. Warner Brothers, 1955 (c). *John Ford* and *Mervyn LeRoy*. Sp: Frank Nugent and Joshua Logan, b/o play by Thomas Heggen and Joshua Logan. Cast: James Cagney, William Powell, Jack Lemmon, Betsy Palmer, Ward Bond, Phil Carey, Nick Adams.

43. WAR AND PEACE. Paramount, 1956 (c). *King Vidor*. Sp: Bridget Boland, King Vidor, Robert Westerby, Mario Camerini, Ennio De Concini, and Ivo Perilli, b/o novel by Leo Tolstoy. Cast: Audrey Hepburn, Mel Ferrer, Vittorio Gassman, John Mills, Herbert Lom, Oscar Homolka, Anita Ekberg, Helmut Dantine.

44. THE WRONG MAN. Warner Brothers, 1956. *Alfred Hitchcock*. Sp: Maxwell Anderson and Angus MacPhail, b/o story by Maxwell Anderson. Cast: Vera Miles, Anthony Quayle, Harold J. Stone, Charles Cooper, Esther Minciotti.

45. 12 ANGRY MEN. An Orion-Nova Production, released by United Artists, 1957. *Sidney Lumet.* Sp: Reginald Rose, b/o on his television play. Cast: Lee J. Cobb, Ed Begley, E.G. Marshall, Jack Warden, Martin Balsam, John Fiedler, Jack Klugman, Edward Binns, Joseph Sweeney, George Voskovec, Robert Webber.

46. THE TIN STAR. Paramount, 1957. *Anthony Mann.* Sp: Dudley Nichols, b/o story by Barney Slater and Joel Kane. Cast: Anthony Perkins, Betsy Palmer, Michel Ray, Neville Brand, John McIntire.

47. STAGE STRUCK. RKO-Buena Vista, 1958 (c). *Sidney Lumet.* Sp: Ruth and Augustus Goetz, b/o play *Morning Glory* by Zoe Akins. Cast: Susan Strasberg, Joan Greenwood, Christopher Plummer, Herbert Marshall, Sally Gracie. Previously filmed in 1933 as *Morning Glory.*

48. WARLOCK. 20th Century-Fox, 1959 (c). *Edward Dmytryk.* Sp: Robert Alan Aurthur, b/o novel by Oakley Hall. Cast: Richard Widmark, Anthony Quinn, Dorothy Malone, Dolores Michaels, Wallace Ford, Tom Drake, Richard Arlen.

49. THE MAN WHO UNDERSTOOD WOMEN. 20th Century-Fox, 1959 (c). *Nunnally Johnson.* Sp: Nunnally Johnson, b/o novel *The Colors of the Day* by Romain Gary. Cast: Leslie Caron, Cesare Danova, Myron McCormick, Marcel Dalio, Conrad Nagel.

50. ADVISE AND CONSENT. Columbia, 1962. *Otto Preminger.* Sp: Wendell Mayes, b/o novel by Allen Drury. Cast: Charles Laughton, Don Murray, Walter Pidgeon, Franchot Tone, Peter Lawford, Lew Ayres, Burgess Meredith, Gene Tierney, Paul Ford, Eddie Hodges, George Grizzard, Inga Swenson.

51. THE LONGEST DAY. 20th Century-Fox, 1962. *Andrew Marton, Ken Annakin,* and *Bernhard Wicki* . Sp: Cornelius Ryan, b/o his book. Cast: John Wayne, Robert Mitchum, Robert Ryan, Richard Todd, Red Buttons, Richard Beymer, Mel Ferrer, Rod Steiger.

52. HOW THE WEST WAS WON. MGM, 1963 (c). *John Ford, George Marshall* and *Henry Hathaway.* Sp: James R Webb, b/o *Life* magazine series. Cast: James Stewart, Debbie Reynolds, Carroll Baker, George Peppard, Gregory Peck, Richard Widmark, John Wayne, Raymond Massey, Lee J. Cobb.

53. SPENCER'S MOUNTAIN. Warner Brothers, 1963 (c). *Delmer Daves.* Sp: Delmer Daves, b/o novel by Earl Hamner, Jr. Cast: Maureen O'Hara, James MacArthur, Donald Crisp, Wally Cox, Mimsy Farmer.

54. FAIL SAFE. Columbia, 1964. *Sidney Lumet*. Sp: Walter Bernstein, b/o novel by Eugene Burdick and Harvey Wheeler. Cast: Dan O'Herlihy, Walter Matthau, Frank Overton, Fritz Weaver, Edward Binns, Larry Hagman.

55. THE BEST MAN. A Millar-Turman-Schaffner Production, released by United Artists, 1964. *Franklin J. Schaffner*. Sp: Gore Vidal, b/o his play. Cast: Cliff Robertson, Lee Tracy, Edie Adams, Margaret Leighton, Ann Sothern, Gene Raymond, Kevin McCarthy, Shelley Berman.

56. SEX AND THE SINGLE GIRL. Warner Brothers, 1964 (c). *Richard Quine*. Sp: Joseph Heller and David R. Schwartz, from a story by Joseph Hoffman, b/o book by Helen Gurley Brown. Cast: Natalie Wood, Tony Curtis, Lauren Bacall, Mel Ferrer, Edward Everett Horton.

57. THE ROUNDERS. MGM, 1965 (c). *Burt Kennedy*. Sp: Burt Kennedy, b/o novel by Max Evans. Cast: Glenn Ford, Chill Wills, Edgar Buchanan, Sue Ane Langdon, Hope Holiday.

58. IN HARM'S WAY. Paramount, 1965. *Otto Preminger*. Sp: Wendell Mayes, b/o novel by James Bassett. Cast: John Wayne, Kirk Douglas, Patricia Neal, Tom Tryon, Paula Prentiss, Brandon de Wilde, Jill Haworth, Dana Andrews.

59. BATTLE OF THE BULGE. Warner Brothers, 1965 (c). *Ken Annakin*. Sp: Philip Yordan, Milton Sperling and John Nelson. Cast: Robert Shaw, Robert Ryan, Dana Andrews, George Montgomery, Telly Savalas, Charles Bronson, Ty Hardin, Pier Angeli, James MacArthur.

60. THE DIRTY GAME (GUERRE SECRET). AIP-Landau-Unger, 1966. *Terence Young, Christian-Jaque,* and *Carlo Lizzani*. Sp: Jo Eisinger, b/o screenplay by Jacques Remy, Christian-Jaque, Ennio de Concini and Philippe Bouvard. Cast: Robert Ryan, Vittorio Gassman, Annie Girardot, Peter Van Eyck.

61. A BIG HAND FOR THE LITTLE LADY. Warner Brothers, 1966 (c). *Fielder Cook*. Sp: Sidney Carroll, b/o his television play, *Big Deal in Laredo*. Cast: Joanne Woodward, Jason Robards, Charles Bickford, Burgess Meredith, Kevin McCarthy, Paul Ford.

62. WELCOME TO HARD TIMES. MGM, 1967 (c). *Burt Kennedy*. Sp: Burt Kennedy, b/o novel by E. L. Doctorow. Cast: Janice Rule, Keenan Wynn, Janis Paige, John Anderson, Warren Oates, Fay Spain, Edgar Buchanan, Aldo Ray.

63. STRANGER ON THE RUN. Universal (Television movie). 1967. (c) *Don Siegel*. Sp: Dean Riesner, b/o story by Reginald Rose. Cast: Michael Parks, Dan Duryea, Anne Baxter, Sal Mineo, Lloyd Bochner.

64. FIRECREEK. Warners-Seven Arts, 1968 (c). *Vincent McEveety*. Sp: Calvin Clements. Cast: James Stewart, Inger Stevens, Gary Lockwood, Dean Jagger, J. Robert Porter, Ed Begley, Jay C. Flippen, Jack Elam.

65. YOURS, MINE AND OURS. A Desilu-Walden Production, released by United Artists, 1968 (c). *Melville Shavelson*. Sp: Melville Shavelson and Mort Lachman, b/o story by Madelyn Davis and Bob Carroll, Jr. Cast: Lucille Ball, Van Johnson, Tom Bosley, Jennifer Leak, Kevin Burchett.

66. MADIGAN. Universal, 1968 (c). *Don Siegel*. Sp: Henri Simoun (Howard Rodman) and Abraham Polonsky, b/o novel *The Commissioner* by Richard Dougherty. Cast: Richard Widmark, Inger Stevens, Harry Guardino, James Whitmore, Susan Clark, Don Stroud, Michael Dunn, Steve Ihnat, Raymond St. Jacques, Lloyd Gough, Sheree North.

67. THE BOSTON STRANGLER. 20th Century-Fox, 1968 (c). *Richard Fleischer*. Sp: Edward Anhalt, b/o book by Gerold Frank. Cast: Tony Curtis, George Kennedy, Mike Kellin, Hurd Hatfield, Murray Hamilton, Jeff Corey, Sally Kellerman, William Marshall.

68. ONCE UPON A TIME IN THE WEST. Paramount, 1969 (c). *Sergio Leone*. Sp: Sergio Leone and Sergio Donati, b/o story by Dario Argento, Bernardo Bertolucci, and Sergio Leone. Cast: Claudia Cardinale, Jason Robards, Charles Bronson, Frank Wolff, Gabriele Ferzetti, Keenan Wynn, Paola Stoppa, Jack Elam, Woody Strode.

69. TOO LATE THE HERO. Cinerama, 1970 (c). *Robert Aldrich*. Sp: Robert Aldrich and Lukas Heller, b/o story by Robert Aldrich and Robert Sherman. Cast: Michael Caine, Cliff Robertson, Ian Bannen, Harry Andrews, Denholm Elliott.

70. THE CHEYENNE SOCIAL CLUB. National General, 1970 (c). *Gene Kelly*. Sp: James Lee Barrett. Cast: James Stewart, Shirley Jones, Sue Ane Langdon, Elaine Devry, Robert Middleton.

71. THERE WAS A CROOKED MAN. Warner Brothers, 1970 (c). *Joseph L. Mankiewicz*. Sp: David Newman and Robert Benton. Cast: Kirk Douglas, Hume Cronyn, Warren Oates, Burgess Meredith, Arthur O'Connell, Martin Gabel, John Randolph, Michael Blodgett, Claudia McNeil, Lee Grant.

72. SOMETIMES A GREAT NOTION. Universal, 1971 (c). *Paul Newman*. Sp: John Gay, b/o novel by Ken Kesey. Cast: Paul Newman, Lee Remick, Michael Sarrazin, Richard Jaeckel, Linda Lawson, Cliff Potts.

73. DIRECTED BY JOHN FORD (Documentary). The American Film Institute, 1971 (c). *Peter Bogdanovich*. Sp: Peter Bogdanovich. Cast: John Ford, John Wayne, James Stewart.

74. THE SERPENT. Henri Verneuil Productions, 1973 (c). *Henri Verneuil*. Sp: Henri Verneuil and Gilles Perrault, b/o novel by Pierre Nord. Cast: Yul Brynner, Dirk Bogarde, Phillippe Noiret, Michel Bouquet, Martin Held, Farley Granger, Virna Lisi, Robert Alda.

75. ASH WEDNESDAY. Paramount, 1973 (c). *Larry Peerce*. Sp: Jean-Claude Tramont. Cast: Elizabeth Taylor, Helmut Berger, Keith Baxter, Maurice Teynac, Margaret Blye.

76. THE RED PONY. Omnibus Productions (Television movie), 1973 (c). *Robert Totten*. Sp: Robert Totten, b/o novel by John Steinbeck. Cast: Maureen O'Hara, Ben Johnson, Jack Elam.

77. THE ALPHA CAPER. (Television movie), 1973 (c). *Robert Michael Lewis*. Sp: Elroy Schwartz. Cast: Leonard Nimoy, James McEachin, Larry Hagman, John Marley.

78. MY NAME IS NOBODY. Universal, 1974 (c). *Tonino Valerii*. Sp: Ernesto Gastaldi, b/o story by Fulvio Morsella and Ernesto Gastaldi, from idea by Sergio Leone. Cast: Terence Hill, Jean Martin, Piero Lulli, Leo Gordon, R.G. Armstrong, Neil Summers.

79. THE LAST DAYS OF MUSSOLINI. 1975 (c). *Carlo Lizzani*. Cast: Rod Steiger.

# THE BROADWAY APPEARANCES OF HENRY FONDA

*The Game of Love and Death.* 1929. by Romain Rolland.
*I Loved You Wednesday.* 1932. by Molly Ricardel and Richard DuBois.
*Forsaking All Others.* 1933. by Frank Cavett and Edward Roberts.
*New Faces.* 1934. organized by Leonard Sillman.
*The Farmer Takes a Wife.* 1934-35. by Marc Connelly and Frank Elser.
*Blow Ye Winds.* 1937. by Valentine Davies.
*Mister Roberts.* 1948-50. by Joshua Logan and Thomas Heggen.
*Point of No Return.* 1951-52. by Paul Osborn.
*The Caine Mutiny Court-Martial.* 1954. by Herman Wouk.
*Two for the Seesaw.* 1958. by William Gibson.
*Silent Night, Lonely Night.* 1959-60. by Robert Anderson.
*Critic's Choice.* 1960-61. by Ira Levin.
*A Gift of Time.* 1962. by Garson Kanin.
*Generation.* 1965-66. by William Goodhart.
*Our Town.* 1969. by Thornton Wilder.
*Clarence Darrow.* 1974 and 1975. by David W. Rintels.

# INDEX

*Advise and Consent*, 104-105, 106
Agar, John, 62
Albee, Edward, 111
Aldrich, Robert, 114
*All About Eve*, 124
*Alpha Caper, The*, 135
Ameche, Don, 43, 56, 74
*America and Americans*, 55
Anderson, Lindsay, 45
Anderson, Robert, 103
Andrews, Dana, 77, 81, 112
Annabella, 29
*Appointment in Samarra*, 83
Arthur, Jean, 75
*Ash Wednesday*, 135
Atkinson, Brooks, 22

Bacall, Lauren, 114
Ball, Lucille, 76, 131
Bancroft, Anne, 101
Bari, Lynn, 74, 75
Barnes, Clive, 135
Barry, Philip, 17
Barrymore, John, 40
*Battle of Midway, The*, 56
*Battle of the Bulge*, 112
Baxter, Warner, 101
*Becky Sharp*, 26
Begley, Ed, 99, 135
Bel Geddes, Barbara, 81, 103
Bellamy, Ralph, 43

Bennett, Joan, 34, 70
Benton, Robert, 124
*Best Man, The*, 13, 105-108, 109
*Big Hand for the Little Lady, A*, 116-117, 124
*Big Heat, The*, 64
*Big Street, The*, 75-76
Billings, George, 19
*Birds, The*, 96
*Blockade*, 25, 38-39, 41
Blore, Eric, 25
Bogart, Humphrey, 91
Bogdanovich, Peter, 10, 30, 31, 88
Bond, Ward, 59
*Bonnie and Clyde*, 124
*Boston Strangler, The*, 131
Brahm, John, 43
Brando, Dorothy, 17, 19
Brando, Marlon, 17, 87
Brent, George, 37
Brian, Mary, 27
Bronson, Charles, 126
Brown, Helen Gurley, 114
Brynner, Yul, 135
Burdick, Eugene, 108
Burton, Richard, 111

Cagney, James, 88
*Caine Mutiny Court-Martial, The*, 87, 137
*Cannery Row*, 87
Capp, Al, 26
Capra, Frank, 10

Cardinale, Claudia, 126, 128
Carné, Marcel, 79
Caron, Leslie, 101
Carradine, John, 53
Carroll, Madeleine, 38, 39
Carson, Jack, 72
Case, Allen, 103
*Catch-22*, 114
*Chad Hanna*, 66
*Cheyenne Social Club, The*, 122
*Clarence Darrow*, 13, 137-139, 140
Clark, Susan, 130
*Clown, The*, 91
Cobb, Lee J., 99
Coburn, Charles, 67
Coca, Imogene, 21
Colbert, Claudette, 50
*Colors of the Day, The*, 101
*Commissioner, The*, 131
Connelly, Marc, 22
*Coogan's Bluff*, 131
Cook, Fielder, 116, 117
Cooper, Gary, 10, 22, 78
Cooper, Jackie, 64
Corliss, Richard, 67
*Country Girl, The*, 91
Crawford, Joan, 81, 82
Crews, Laura Hope, 19
Crisp, Donald, 34
*Critic's Choice*, 103
Curtis, Tony, 114, 115, 131

*Daisy Kenyon*, 81-82
Darwell, Jane, 53, 55
Daves, Delmer, 110
Davis, Bette, 33, 34, 35, 37, 76, 111
de Havilland, Olivia, 71
De Laurentiis, Dino, 92
Del Rio, Dolores, 59
*Deputy, The*, 103
Dieterle, William, 39
*Directed by John Ford*, 88
*Dirty Game, The*, 112, 114
*Dirty Harry*, 119, 131
Douglas, Kirk, 124
Downs, Cathy, 56
*Dr. Strangelove*, 109
*Drums Along the Mohawk*, 50-51, 66, 140
Drury, Allen, 104
Duvivier, Julien, 75

*Easy Rider*, 139
Edmonds, Walter, 50, 66

*Fail Safe*, 13, 108-110
*Farmer Takes a Wife, The* (film), 10, 23, 45, 50, 66
*Farmer Takes a Wife, The* (play), 22
*Fathers Against Sons Against Fathers*, 137
Faye, Alice, 64
Ferrer, Jose, 87
Fields, Dorothy, 25
Figueroa, Gabriel, 61

Firecreek, 119-120, 122, 128
Fleming, Victor, 23
Flynn, Errol, 35
Fonda, Frances Brokaw, 29, 84
Fonda, Jane, 16, 38, 91, 111, 133, 139
Fonda, Peter, 19, 64, 139
Fonda, Shirlee Adams, 111
Fonda, Susan Blanchard, 86
Fonda, William Brace, 17
Ford, John, 10, 44, 45, 47, 48, 50, 51, 53, 55, 56, 59, 61, 62, 63, 64, 66, 67, 87, 88, 117, 126, 127
Ford, Glenn, 115, 116
Ford, Paul, 116
*Foreign Correspondent*, 39
*Forsaking All Others*, 21
*Fort Apache*, 61-63, 83
*42nd Street*, 101
*Fugitive, The*, 59, 61
*Fury*, 29, 64

*Game of Love and Death, The*, 20
Gary, Romain, 101
Gaynor, Janet, 22, 23, 24
*Generation*, 111
Gibson, William, 101
Gish, Lillian, 24
*Gone With the Wind*, 35
Goodhart, William, 110
Goulding, Edmund, 34

*Grapes of Wrath, The*, 13, 25, 41, 53-55, 59, 64, 76, 77
*Great McGinty, The*, 67
Greene, Graham, 59
Griffith, D.W., 10, 24

Hagman, Larry, 109
Hammerstein, Oscar II, 86
Hamner, Earl, 110
Hathaway, Henry, 26, 40
Hayden, Tom, 140
Hayward, Leland, 21, 25, 83, 87
Hecht, Ben, 135
Heggen, Thomas, 83, 84
Heller, Joseph, 114
Hepburn, Audrey, 92
Hepburn, Katharine, 101
*High Noon*, 95
Hill, Terence, 129
Hitchcock, Alfred, 29, 42, 55, 95, 96, 97
Holden, William, 87
*How the West Was Won*, 112, 122
Hudson, Rochelle, 24
Huston, John, 83

*I Dream Too Much*, 24
*I Loved You Wednesday*, 21
*I Met My Love Again*, 34-35
*Immortal Sergeant, The*, 78, 79
*In Harm's Way*, 112
*Informer, The*, 45, 61

155

Jaeckel, Richard, 133
Jaynes, Herberta, 17
*Jesse James*, 41-42, 53, 64, 66, 128
*Jezebel*, 35, 37-38
*Jigsaw*, 84
*Jour Se Leve, Le (Daybreak)*, 79

Kelly, Emmett, 91
Kennedy, Burt, 115, 117
Kennedy, George, 131
Kern, Jerome, 25
Kerr, Geoffrey, 22
Kerr, Jean, 103
Kerr, Walter, 103, 137
Kesey, Ken, 133
King, Henry, 10, 24, 42
*King Kong*, 76
*Kiss for Cinderella, A*, 21
*Klute*, 139
Kubrick, Stanley, 109

*Lady Eve, The*, 13, 41, 67-70, 74, 92
Lamour, Dorothy, 66
Lang, Fritz, 29, 30, 31, 42, 43, 64, 97, 129
Lang, Walter, 75
Laughton, Charles, 105
Lawson, John Howard, 38
Lemmon, Jack, 88
Leone, Sergio, 120, 126, 127, 128, 129
LeRoy, Mervyn, 88
*Let Us Live*, 42-43, 95

Levin, Ira, 103
*Lillian Russell*, 64
Lindsay, Margaret, 33
Litvak, Anatole, 79
Logan, Joshua, 19, 35, 83, 84
*Long Night, The*, 79-81
*Longest Day, The*, 112
Louise, Anita, 34
Lumet, Sidney, 98, 99, 100, 109

*M*, 30
MacArthur, Charles, 135
MacArthur, James, 110
MacMurray, Fred, 25
*Mad Miss Manton, The*, 40-41
*Madigan*, 119, 130-131
*Magnificent Dope, The*, 74-75
*Male Animal, The*, 71-72, 91
*Man Who Shot Liberty Valance, The*, 63
*Man Who Understood Women, The*, 101, 103
Mankiewicz, Joseph L., 124
Mann, Anthony, 94
Marquand, J.P., 86
Marshall, E.G., 100
Mature, Victor, 56
McCormick, Myron, 19
McCrea, Joel, 22, 39
McGuire, Dorothy, 21, 91
Menjou, Adolphe, 100
*Merton of the Movies*, 19
Miles, Vera, 97

*Miracle Can Happen, A (On Our Merry Way)*, 82, 122
*Mister Roberts* (film), 15, 63, 87, 88-90, 130, 135
*Mister Roberts* (play), 83, 84-86, 87
Mitchell, Thomas, 78
*Moon's Our Home, The*, 26
Morgan, Henry, 77
*Morning Glory*, 100
Morricone, Ennio, 127, 129
*Mr. Deeds Goes to Town*, 74
*Mr. President*, 108
*Mr. Smith Goes to Washington*, 55
*My Darling Clementine*, 13, 56-59, 66, 79
*My Name is Nobody*, 129-130

Naish, J. Carrol, 59
Natwick, Mildred, 19, 135
*New Faces of 1934*, 21
Newman, Paul, 133
Nichols, Dudley, 61, 95
*North by Northwest*, 96
Nugent, Elliott, 71

O'Brien, Pat, 31
Odets, Clifford, 91
O'Hara, John, 83
O'Hara, Maureen, 78, 110
*Once Upon a Time in the West*, 126-129, 140
Osborn, Paul, 86
O'Sullivan, Maureen, 42

*Our Town*, 135, 137
*Ox-Bow Incident, The*, 13, 76-78, 93, 100

Palmer, Betsy, 94
Parks, Michael, 119
*Parrish*, 110
Paterson, Pat, 27
Penn, Arthur, 29
Peppard, George, 112
Perkins, Anthony, 94, 95, 97
*Petrified Forest, The*, 91
*Philadelphia Story, The*, 55
Platt, Louise, 40
*Point of No Return*, 86-87
Pons, Lily, 24, 25
*Potemkin*, 39
Powell, William, 90
*Power and the Glory, The*, 59
Power, Tyrone, 41, 42, 44, 56
Preminger, Otto, 81, 104, 106, 112
Price, Vincent, 81
*Psycho*, 96, 97

Quinn, Anthony, 95

Raft, George, 40
*Rancho Notorious*, 64
Ray, Aldo, 117
*Rebecca*, 55
*Red Pony, The*, 55

*Return of Frank James, The*, 64-66
*Rings on Her Fingers*, 74
Rintels, David W., 137
*Rio Grande*, 61
Ripley, Arthur, 35
Robertson, Cliff, 107, 114
Rogers, Ginger, 75
Romero, Cesar, 75
Rose, Reginald, 98
*Rounders, The*, 115-116, 117
Rule, Janice, 117
Runyon, Damon, 76
Ryan, Robert, 114, 135

Saroyan, William, 137
Sarrazin, Michael, 133
Sarris, Andrew, 48, 119
Schaffner, Franklin, 105
Schickel, Richard, 13
Scott, Martha, 135
*Seesaw Log, The*, 101
Selznick, David O., 35
Sennwald, André, 23
*Serpent, The*, 135
*Seven Days in May*, 108
*Sex and the Single Girl*, 114-115
*Shane*, 95
Shavelson, Melville, 132
*She Wore a Yellow Ribbon*, 61
Sidney, Sylvia, 25, 26, 29
Siegel, Don, 119, 130, 131

*Silent Night, Lonely Night*, 103
*Slim*, 31, 33, 39
"Smith Family, The," 132-133
Smith, Kent, 19
*Sometimes a Great Notion*, 133-135
*Spawn of the North*, 39-40
*Spencer's Mountain*, 110-111, 131, 132
*Spendthrift*, 27, 71
*Stage Struck*, 100-101
Stanwyck, Barbara, 40, 41, 67, 69, 71
Steinbeck, John, 55, 56, 87
Stevens, George, 83
Stewart, James, 10, 16, 19, 55, 82, 97, 115, 120, 122, 123
*Story of Alexander Graham Bell, The*, 43-44
*Stranger on the Run*, 117, 119
Strasberg, Susan, 100, 101
Sturges, Preston, 67, 68, 74
Sullavan, Margaret, 19, 21, 26
*Sullivan's Travels*, 67
*Summer Place, A*, 110
*Swan, The*, 22
Swanson, Gloria, 34

*Tales of Manhattan*, 75
Taylor, Elizabeth, 111, 135
Temple, Shirley, 62
*That Certain Woman*, 33-34, 35, 76
*There Was a Crooked Man*, 123-124
*Thin Man, The*, 40
Thurber, James, 71

Tierney, Gene, 64, 74
*Time of Your Life, The*, 137
*Tin Star, The*, 93-95
Toland, Gregg, 55
Tone, Franchot, 84
*Too Late the Hero*, 114
Tracy, Lee, 107
*Trail of the Lonesome Pine, The*, 24, 25-26, 27, 40, 110
*Travels with Charley*, 55
*Trespasser, The*, 34
Trotti, Lamar, 45
Truffaut, Francois, 95
*12 Angry Men*, 13, 98-100, 112
*Two for the Seesaw*, 101

Valerii, Tonino, 129
*Vertigo*, 96, 97
Vidal, Gore, 105, 108
Vidor, King, 10, 92

Walker, June, 22
Walsh, Raoul, 27
*Waltons, The*, 110
Wanger, Walter, 21, 23, 25, 26, 29, 34, 38, 39, 56
*War and Peace*, 92-93
*Warlock*, 95, 128
*Way Down East*, 23
Wayne, David, 88
Wayne, John, 16, 62, 63, 112, 115

*Welcome to Hard Times*, 117, 119
Wellman, William, 76
Wheeler, Harvey, 108
Whitmore, James, 130
*Who's Afraid of Virginia Woolf?*, 111
Widmark, Richard, 95, 131
*Wild Geese Calling*, 70
Wilder, Thornton, 135
Windust, Bretaigne, 19
*Wings of the Morning*, 27, 29
*Wizard of Oz, The*, 21
Wood, Natalie, 114
Woodward, Joanne, 116
Wouk, Herman, 87
*Wrong Man, The*, 29, 42, 95-98
Wyler, William, 26, 37

*You and I*, 17
*You Belong to Me*, 71
*You Only Live Once*, 13, 29-31, 42, 43, 53, 95, 97
*Young Mr. Lincoln*, 13, 23, 29, 43, 44, 45-48, 49, 50, 56, 66, 137
Young, Terence, 112
*Yours, Mine and Ours*, 131-132

Zanuck, Darryl F., 43, 45, 56, 64, 70, 74, 76, 112

*ABOUT THE AUTHOR*
Michael Kerbel is an Assistant Professor of Cinema at the University of Bridgeport. He has written extensively on film for *The Village Voice* and *Film Comment*, and is the author of *Paul Newman*, a Pyramid Illustrated History of the Movies.

*ABOUT THE EDITOR*
Ted Sennett is the author of *Warner Brothers Presents*, a tribute to the great Warners films of the Thirties and Forties, and of *Lunatics and Lovers*, on the long-vanished but well-remembered "screwball" comedies of the past. He is also the editor of *The Movie Buff's Book* and has written about films for magazines and newspapers. He lives in New Jersey with his wife and three children.